Exploring Science

How Science Works

7

Series Editor:
Mark Levesley

Penny Johnson
Steve Gray

PEARSON
Longman

Edinburgh Gate
Harlow, Essex

This book also includes
Active Book

D0183862

Contents

How to use this book

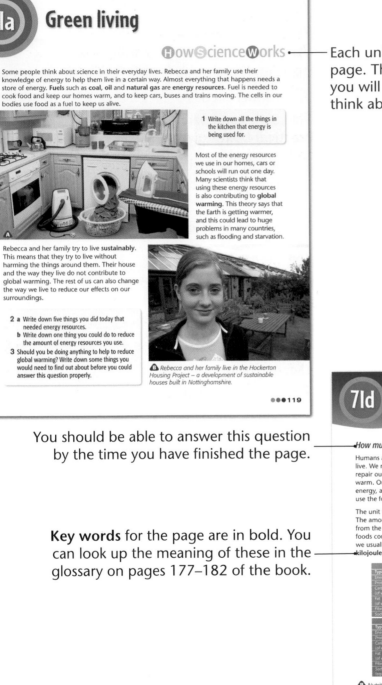

7Ia Green living

HowScienceWorks

Some people think about science in their everyday lives. Rebecca and her family use their knowledge of energy to help them live in a certain way. Almost everything that happens needs a store of energy. **Fuels** such as **coal**, **oil** and **natural gas** are **energy resources**. Fuel is needed to cook food and keep our homes warm, and to keep cars, buses and trains moving. The cells in our bodies use food as a fuel to keep us alive.

1 Write down all the things in the kitchen that energy is being used for.

Most of the energy resources we use in our homes, cars or schools will run out one day. Many scientists think that using these energy resources is also contributing to **global warming**. This theory says that the Earth is getting warmer, and this could lead to huge problems in many countries, such as flooding and starvation.

Rebecca and her family try to live **sustainably**. This means that they try to live without harming the things around them. Their house and the way they live do not contribute to global warming. The rest of us can also change the way we live to reduce our effects on our surroundings.

2 a Write down five things you did today that needed energy resources.
　b Write down one thing you could do to reduce the amount of energy resources you use.
3 Should you be doing anything to help to reduce global warming? Write down some things you would need to find out about before you could answer this question properly.

Rebecca and her family live in the Hockerton Housing Project – a development of sustainable houses built in Nottinghamshire.

●●●119

Each unit starts with a 'How Science Works' page. This introduces some of the ideas that you will learn more about, by making you think about a real-life situation.

You should be able to answer this question by the time you have finished the page.

Key words for the page are in bold. You can look up the meaning of these in the glossary on pages 177–182 of the book.

Timeline boxes tell you about how the work of scientists has developed over time.

Fact boxes contain fascinating facts to think about.

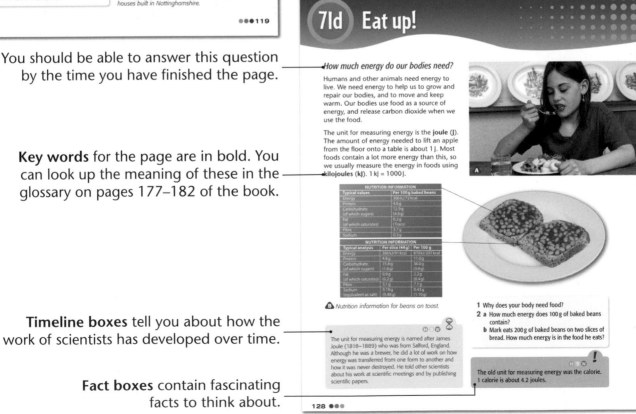

7Id Eat up!

How much energy do our bodies need?

Humans and other animals need energy to live. We need energy to help us to grow and repair our bodies, and to move and keep warm. Our bodies use food as a source of energy, and release carbon dioxide when we use the food.

The unit for measuring energy is the **joule** (J). The amount of energy needed to lift an apple from the floor onto a table is about 1 J. Most foods contain a lot more energy than this, so we usually measure the energy in foods using **kilojoules** (**kJ**). 1 kJ = 1000 J.

NUTRITION INFORMATION	
Typical values	Per 100 g baked beans
Energy	306kJ/72 kcal
Protein	4.6g
Carbohydrate	12.9g
(of which sugars)	(4.8g)
Fat	0.2g
(of which saturates)	(Trace)
Fibre	3.7g
Sodium	0.3g

NUTRITION INFORMATION		
Typical analysis	Per slice (44g)	Per 100 g
Energy	386kJ/91 kcal	878kJ/207 kcal
Protein	4.8g	11.0g
Carbohydrate	15.8g	36.0g
(of which sugars)	(1.6g)	(3.8g)
Fat	0.9g	2.2g
(of which saturates)	(0.2g)	(0.4g)
Fibre	3.1g	7.1g
Sodium	0.19g	0.43g
(equivalent as salt)	(0.48g)	(1.10g)

B Nutrition information for beans on toast.

1 Why does your body need food?
2 a How much energy does 100 g of baked beans contain?
　b Mark eats 200 g of baked beans on two slices of bread. How much energy is in the food he eats?

The unit for measuring energy is named after James Joule (1818–1889) who was from Salford, England. Although he was a brewer, he did a lot of work on how energy was transferred from one form to another and how it was never destroyed. He told other scientists about his work at scientific meetings and by publishing scientific papers.

The old unit for measuring energy was the calorie. 1 calorie is about 4.2 joules.

128 ●●●

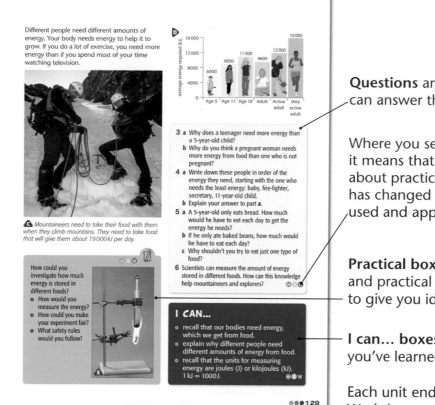

Different people need different amounts of energy. Your body needs energy to help it to grow. If you do a lot of exercise, you need more energy than if you spend most of your time watching television.

⚠️ *Mountaineers need to take their food with them when they climb mountains. They need to take food that will give them about 19 000 kJ per day.*

How could you investigate how much energy is stored in different foods?
- How would you measure the energy?
- How could you make your experiment fair?
- What safety rules would you follow?

3 a Why does a teenager need more energy than a 5-year-old child?
b Why do you think a pregnant woman needs more energy from food than one who is not pregnant?
4 a Write down these people in order of the energy they need, starting with the one who needs the least energy: baby, fire-fighter, secretary, 11-year-old child.
b Explain your answer to part **a**.
5 a A 5-year-old only eats bread. How much would he have to eat each day to get the energy he needs?
b If he only ate baked beans, how much would he have to eat each day?
c Why shouldn't you try to eat just one type of food?
6 Scientists can measure the amount of energy stored in different foods. How can this knowledge help mountaineers and explorers?

I CAN...
- recall that our bodies need energy, which we get from food.
- explain why different people need different amounts of energy from food.
- recall that the units for measuring energy are joules (J) or kilojoules (kJ). 1 kJ = 1000 J.

●●●129

Questions are spread throughout the page so you can answer them as you go through the topic.

Where you see this How Science Works icon, it means that the question or piece of text is about practical or enquiry skills, how science has changed over time, or how science is used and applied in real-life.

Practical boxes give you ideas for investigations and practical work. Sometimes there is a picture to give you ideas for planning your investigation.

I can... boxes help you to assess what you've learned and check your progress.

Each unit ends with a 'How Science Works' page. Here you can apply what you've learned to a real-life situation.

These give you extra information about the topic.

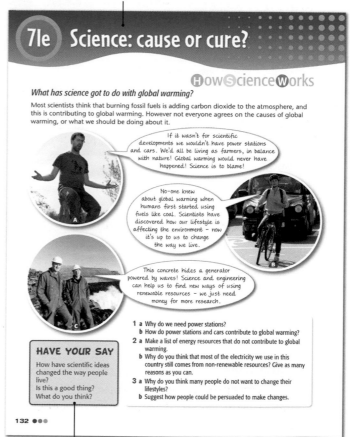

7Ic Focus on: Using energy resources

What are the advantages and disadvantages of our energy resources?

A A geothermal power station

Energy resource	Advantages	Disadvantages
geothermal	clean, cheap, renewable	It is only possible in certain parts of the world where hot rocks are near the surface of the Earth.
burning fossil fuels	cheap	non-renewable It produces carbon dioxide which causes global warming.
nuclear	It does not produce harmful gases.	expensive, non-renewable It produces dangerous radioactive substances that are difficult to get rid of.
solar	clean, renewable	No electricity is produced at night or if there is little sun. Solar panels do not collect very much heat energy. Solar cells are expensive and take up a lot of space.
hydroelectric	clean, renewable	Reservoirs take up huge amounts of space and destroy countryside. It only works in wet mountain regions.
wind	clean, renewable	Electricity is not produced if there is no wind. Wind turbines are noisy and many of them are needed to make useful amounts of electricity. Some people think that they spoil the countryside.
wave	clean, renewable	It does not produce very much electricity. It will not work in calm waters.
tidal	clean, renewable	It only works on some rivers. Dams across the rivers can affect wildlife. Tidal generators at sea could affect fish or shipping.
biomass	renewable It adds less carbon dioxide to the atmosphere than burning fossil fuels.	It may still add some carbon dioxide to the atmosphere. It needs large areas of land to grow crops.

1 Which of the renewable energy resources would be best to use in your area? Explain why.
2 Which of the renewable energy resources would be useless in your area? Explain why.
3 It costs a lot to build nuclear or hydroelectric power stations. Which energy resources would be best for countries that do not have a lot of money?
4 Your next-door neighbours want to put a wind turbine on their roof.
a How could this affect you?
b How could they use renewable energy resources in a way that would affect their neighbours less?

●●●127

If you need to find information about something, use the **index** on pages 183–184.

7Ie Science: cause or cure?

How Science Works

What has science got to do with global warming?

Most scientists think that burning fossil fuels is adding carbon dioxide to the atmosphere, and this is contributing to global warming. However not everyone agrees on the causes of global warming, or what we should be doing about it.

If it wasn't for scientific developments we wouldn't have power stations and cars. We'd all be living as farmers, in balance with nature! Global warming would never have happened! Science is to blame!

No-one knew about global warming when humans first started using fuels like coal. Scientists have discovered how our lifestyle is affecting the environment – now it's up to us to change the way we live.

This concrete hides a generator powered by waves! Science and engineering can help us to find new ways of using renewable resources – we just need money for more research.

HAVE YOUR SAY

How have scientific ideas changed the way people live?
Is this a good thing?
What do you think?

1 a Why do we need power stations?
b How do power stations and cars contribute to global warming?
2 a Make a list of energy resources that do not contribute to global warming.
b Why do you think that most of the electricity we use in this country still comes from non-renewable resources? Give as many reasons as you can.
3 a Why do you think many people do not want to change their lifestyles?
b Suggest how people could be persuaded to make changes.

132 ●●●

The **Have your say box** gives you an issue for a debate or discussion

●●●5

How to use this ActiveBook

Click on this tab to find all the electronic files on the ActiveBook.

Click this tab to see all the key words and what they mean. You can read them or you can click 'play' and listen to someone else read them out for you, to help with pronunciation.

Click on this tab at any time to search for help on how to use the ActiveBook.

Click on a section of the page and it will magnify, so that you can read it easily on screen. You can also zoom in on photos and diagrams on the page.

All of the questions in your book come with a level and some example answers, so you can see exactly how you're doing and how to improve. These are on your teacher's CD-ROM version of the book.

Click on any of the words in **bold** to see a box with the word and what it means. You can read them or you can click 'play' and listen to someone else read them out for you to help with pronunciation.

You can choose to see the pages of the book turn, or not.

Click this button to see all the links to electronic files. If you don't want to see these links you can return to book view.

Click these buttons to view the page as a single page or a double page.

Click here to return to the contents page, or go back to the start of the unit.

You can turn to one page at a time, or you can type in the number of the page and go straight to that page. You can go to the end of the book by clicking ▶︎.

How Science Works

Abbey had a **heart transplant** six years ago because she had a disease called cardio myopathy. She is now fit and healthy again.

In the 1950s an American surgeon called James Hardy (1918–2003) carried out heart transplants in animals. Then in 1964 he put a chimpanzee heart into a man. The heart beat for only 90 minutes and the patient died. Hardy said, however, that the operation showed it was possible to put new hearts into humans.

In 1967, South African surgeon Christiaan Barnard (1922–2001) gave a man the heart of a woman who had died in a road accident. The man survived for 18 days. Two weeks later, Barnard did another heart transplant operation. This patient survived for 18 months.

Today about 300 heart transplants are done in the UK every year and about 70% of these patients live for at least another 5 years. Many people carry donor cards so that if they die, their organs can be used in transplant operations.

A Abbey.

Daily Mirror — Car-crash victim saves a life

DYING MAN GETS SPARE HEART

ALL SET FOR RAIL CHAOS

A hospital team make history

THE GIRL WHO DIED

NDFS

B

!
The longest surviving heart transplant patient is Tony Huesman who received a new heart in 1978 when he was 20.

Donor Card
I would like to help someone to live after my death.
Let your relatives know your wishes.

c

1 Why do you think Hardy carried out heart transplants in animals?

2 How did most people find out about the news of Barnard's operation?

3 a In the 1960s many people were against heart transplants. Suggest a reason why.

   b Today most people are in favour of heart transplants. What has happened to change people's views?

4 Some people think that people should carry cards only if they don't want to donate their organs – the opposite of donor cards. What do you think of this idea?

Human organs

What are the main organs in a human?

The heart is an **organ**. Every organ has a **function** (a job to do).

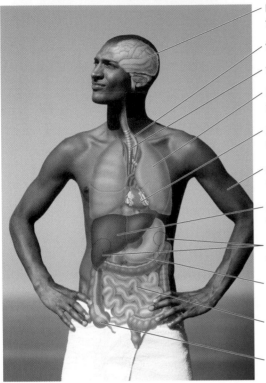

brain
to control the body

foodpipe (**gullet**)

windpipe (**trachea**)

lungs
for breathing

heart
to pump blood

skin
for protection and feeling

liver
to make and destroy substances

kidneys (at back)
to clean the blood and make urine

stomach
to break up food

small intestine
to break up food and absorb it

large intestine
to remove water from unwanted food

A *Some of the organs in your body.*

Many organs can be transplanted, including skin. The first skin transplants were carried out in India 5000 years ago. In 2005, French doctors transplanted a face onto Isabelle Dinoire, whose nose and mouth had been bitten off by a dog.

H S W !

B

1 Draw a table to show the functions of five different organs.

2 a Which organ makes urine?
   b Which organ gets bigger as it fills with air?
   c Name three organs that food passes through.

3 a Suggest one problem that Isabelle Dinoire may have had after her operation. H S W
   b Do you think face transplants should be allowed? Give a reason for your answer. H S W

I CAN...

o recall information about all the organs on this page, where they are and what they do.

o draw a table to show information. H S W

What are organs made from?

Photo A shows a human heart. You can see that it is made from different parts. The yellowy parts are fat and the reddish parts are muscle. These parts are known as **tissues**.

> **1** Name two tissues found in the heart.

Like all organs, the heart is made of different tissues. You can see some of the tissues, for example fat tissue, but not others, such as nerve tissue. The heart has a very important function; it pumps blood around the body to supply all our tissues with food and oxygen.

> **2** What is the function of the heart?

Plants also have organs made out of tissues. For example, roots are covered with **root hair tissue** and inside them there is **xylem tissue** (pronounced '*zy-lem*') which carries water.

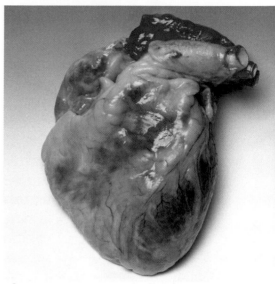

A The heart is made of different tissues.

Tissues (e.g. bone) can also be transplanted. About 1000 bone transplants are done in the UK each year.

> **3 a** In which organ does a plant make its food?
> **b** Which organ contains root hair tissue?
> **c** Apart from the root, name a plant organ that contains xylem tissue.

flower for reproduction

leaf makes food for the plant (using **photosynthesis**)

stem carries substances around the plant and holds the leaves in place

root takes water out of the soil and holds the plant in the ground

root hair tissue

B Some organs in a plant.

I CAN...

- state that organs are made from tissues.
- recall the main plant organs and what they do.

How do we use a microscope?

To find out what is wrong with an organ, doctors do tests. Some tests involve taking a small part of the organ (a **biopsy**) and having a look at it under a **microscope**. Microscopes make things appear much bigger than they actually are. They **magnify** things.

fine focusing wheel

1 Place the smallest **objective lens** (the lowest **magnification**) over the hole in the stage. Turn the **coarse focusing wheel** to make the gap between the objective lens and the stage as small as possible.

objective lenses

coarse focusing wheel

stage

2 Place the **slide** under the clips on the **stage**. This contains the **specimen** (the thing you want to look at). Then adjust the light source so that light goes up through the hole.

light source

slide

specimen

3 Look through the **eyepiece lens**. Turn the coarse focusing wheel slowly until what you see is in **focus** (clear and sharp).

4 To see a bigger **image**, place the next largest objective lens over your specimen.

5 Use the **fine focusing wheel** to get your image in focus again. Do not use the coarse focusing wheel since you can break the slide and damage the objective lens. If you can't see clearly what you are looking for go back to a lower magnification.

⚠ Never point the mirror directly at the Sun. This can permanently damage your eyesight.

1 Jake sets up a microscope but can only see darkness when looking into the eyepiece lens. What might be wrong? Write down as many things that could be wrong as you can think of.

2 Write down some rules of your own for: Ⓗ Ⓢ Ⓦ
   a using a microscope safely
   b taking care of a microscope.

Ⓗ Ⓢ Ⓦ

In 1590 a spectacles maker from Holland, called Zacharias Janssen, placed two lenses into a tube and invented the microscope.

I CAN...

o use a microscope to view slides. Ⓗ Ⓢ Ⓦ

How can we prepare things to look at with a microscope?

The specimen on a microscope slide needs to be thin so that light can pass through it. A **coverslip** is a thin piece of glass that goes over the specimen to keep it flat, hold it in place and stop it drying out.

1 What is a specimen?
2 Why does a specimen need to be thin?

A *The specimen in the top slide is too thick.*

Onions are plant organs that grow underground. The plant uses them to store food. But what are onions made of? You are going to investigate this by making a slide.

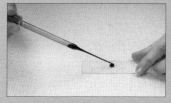  

1 Take a slide and place a drop of water in the centre. The water may contain a **stain** to make the specimen show up better.

2 Use some forceps to peel off the inside layer of a piece of onion.

3 Place your onion skin onto the drop of water on your slide.

4 Use some forceps to lower a coverslip onto your specimen. If you do this carefully and slowly you will not get air bubbles trapped under the coverslip.

 Slides and coverslips are made of thin glass. Be very careful when you are using them.

When you have finished, write a report to explain how you prepared your slide, including:
- any problems you had
- what sort of stain you used and why
- a labelled drawing of one or two of your cells
- another question that could be answered by using a microscope.

3 Why do we use coverslips?
4 A microscope has a ×10 eyepiece lens and a ×15 objective lens. What is its total magnification?

When using a microscope, we need to know what **magnification** we are using. Both the eyepiece lens and the objective lens do some magnifying. How much each lens magnifies is written on its side (e.g. ×10).

$$\frac{\text{total}}{\text{magnification}} = \frac{\text{magnification of}}{\text{the eyepiece lens}} \times \frac{\text{magnification of}}{\text{the objective lens}}$$

I CAN...
- prepare a microscope slide. H S W

What are plant and animal cells?

The first person to use a microscope to look at part of a plant was Robert Hooke. In about 1665 he looked at some cork tissue and noticed what he thought looked like small rooms. He called them **cells**. Today we know that all tissues are made of cells and that there are animal cells and plant cells. Our bodies contain over 1 000 000 000 000 animal cells!

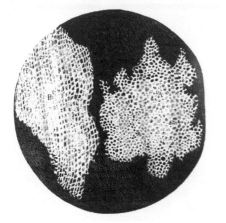

eyepiece lens

focusing ring

objective lens

B Hooke's drawing of cork cells. He published this in his book Micrographia *for others to see.*

C A reproduction of Hooke's microscope.

A *Robert Hooke (1635–1703).*

1 Why did Hooke call the boxes he saw in the cork 'cells'? **H S W**

2 How did Hooke tell others about his discovery? **H S W**

Today's microscopes allow us to see cells in great detail. The drawing below shows the parts of an animal cell. The photograph shows a cell taken from inside someone's cheek.

3 How many cells are shown in photograph D?

4 a What does the nucleus do?
  b State two functions of the cell surface membrane.
  c What happens in the cytoplasm?

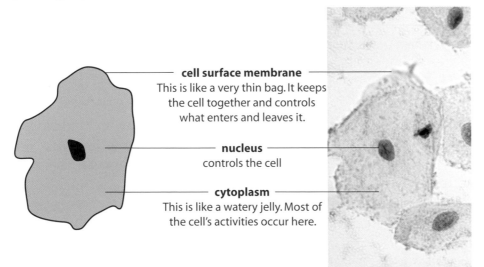

cell surface membrane
This is like a very thin bag. It keeps the cell together and controls what enters and leaves it.

nucleus
controls the cell

cytoplasm
This is like a watery jelly. Most of the cell's activities occur here.

D *Animal cells (magnification ×1000).*

H S W

You can obtain some cells by touching the inside of your cheek.
○ How would you find out what your cheek cells look like?
○ How will you tell others about what you find?

Plant cells share some similarities with animal cells. They both have cytoplasm, a nucleus and a cell surface membrane. However, they do have some differences. Plant cells have straighter edges and are more box-shaped. These cells are from a moss leaf.

An average animal cell is about 0.02 mm across. An average plant cell is about 0.04 mm across. Cell surface membranes are only 0.000 01 mm thick.

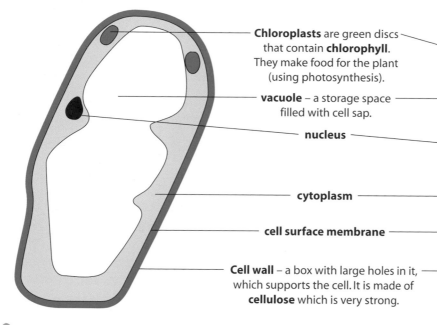

Chloroplasts are green discs that contain **chlorophyll**. They make food for the plant (using photosynthesis).

vacuole – a storage space filled with cell sap.

nucleus

cytoplasm

cell surface membrane

Cell wall – a box with large holes in it, which supports the cell. It is made of **cellulose** which is very strong.

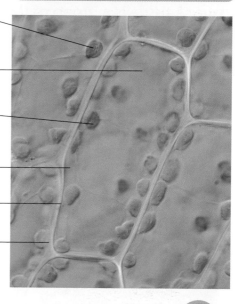

E *Plant cells (magnification ×600).*

5 Write down the cell parts that only plant cells have.
6 What makes plant cells green?
7 a Draw a basic line diagram of a plant cell and label all of its parts.
  b Make a table to explain what each part of the plant cell does.

H S W

Hooke's microscope had a magnification of about ×30. Today's most power microscopes have magnifications of around ×50 000 000!

The animal cell in the photograph on the opposite page is 1000 times bigger than in real life. It has been magnified 1000 times. We say it has a magnification of ×1000.

8 Think of a plus, a minus, and an interesting point about these statements:
  a Cells should be bigger.
  b Cell membranes should be thicker.
9 a Measure the widest part of the animal cell on the previous page. Now work out its width in real life.
  b Work out the length of the plant cell in real life.
10 Think of a scientific question you could answer by using a microscope. **H S W**

I CAN...

o list the parts of animal and plant cells and describe what they do.
o explain how advances in technology allow advances in scientific understanding. **H S W**

Why do cells have different shapes?

Cells of the same type that are grouped together form a tissue. A tissue is a group of the same sort of cells, all working together to do a job.

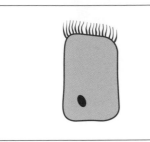

A *A **ciliated epithelial cell**. The strands at the top (**cilia**) wave about to move things.*

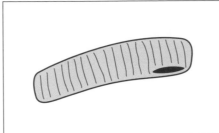

B *A **muscle cell** is able to change length.*

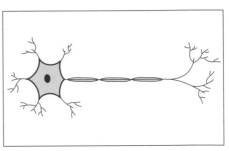

C *A **nerve cell** (**neuron**) can be very long so that signals can be carried around the body very quickly (at speeds of over 400 km/h).*

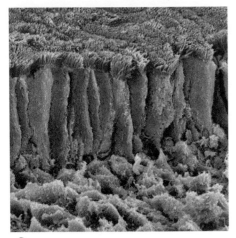

D *Ciliated epithelial tissue in a lung. The cilia wave together to move dirt out of the lungs (magnification ×1500).*

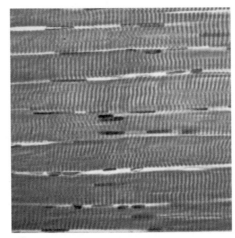

E *Muscle tissue allows us to move (magnification ×4).*

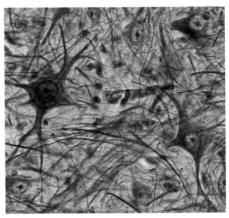

F *Nerve tissue in the brain (magnification ×120–3000).*

You can see that many cells have special shapes that help with their functions. We say that cells are **adapted** to their functions. Some cells look uninteresting but are adapted in other ways. Islet (pronounced '*eye-let*') cells in an organ called the pancreas produce a chemical called insulin. No other cells do this. In people with diabetes these cells do not work. It is hoped that this disease could be treated by using islet cell transplants.

2 Why are nerve cells so long?
3 In what organ would you expect to find the most nerve tissue?
4 Cigarette smoke stops cilia from working. **H S W**
  a How will this affect a smoker's lungs?
  b Use this idea to draw a poster that might help to convince smokers to quit.

Plant cells also come in different shapes and sizes.

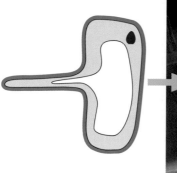
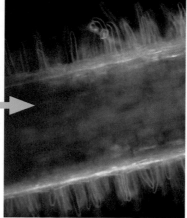

G A **root hair cell** takes water out of the ground quickly. The root hair gives the water more surface area to get into the root.

Root hair tissue (stained orange) (magnification ×25).

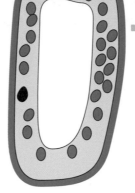
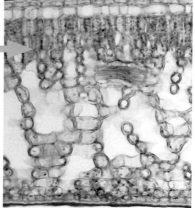

H **Palisade cells** are packed with chloroplasts to help make food for the plant.

Palisade tissue forms a layer near the top of the leaf (magnification ×25).

5 a Which process, needing light, happens in palisade cells?
  b Which part of a palisade cell does this happen in?

6 a What does a root hair cell do?
  b How does its shape help it to do this?
  c What does a palisade cell have that a root hair cell does not? **H S W**
  d Explain this difference.

7 Picture I shows a xylem cell.
  a How are xylem cells adapted to carry water?
  b What do you think a group of these cells is called?

8 Which is the odd one out and why?
  muscle cell   palisade cell   root hair cell   xylem cell

9 The improvement to what piece of equipment allowed Schwann to find cells in all organisms? **H S W**

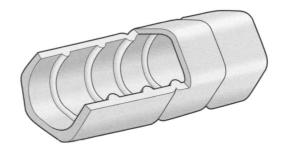

 This is a **xylem cell**. Xylem cells join together to form hollow tubes, which carry water.

H S W

In 1839 German scientist Theodor Schwann (1810–1882) published his **theory** that cells were the smallest living units from which all organisms were made. Before this time many scientists thought that tissues were the smallest parts.

I CAN...

o recall that a group of the same sort of cells is called a tissue.

o describe how ciliated epithelial cells, nerve cells and root hair cells are adapted to their functions.

o explain how the theory that all organisms are made of cells is supported by evidence from microscopes. **H S W**

How are new cells made?

For something to be alive it must move, reproduce, sense things, grow, respire, **excrete** (get rid of waste), and need **nutrition** (food). Cells do all these seven 'life processes' and they help whole organisms to do them too.

All living things grow. For whole plants and animals to get bigger, they need to make more cells. The cells need to reproduce. They do this by **cell division**, when one cell splits to make two new cells.

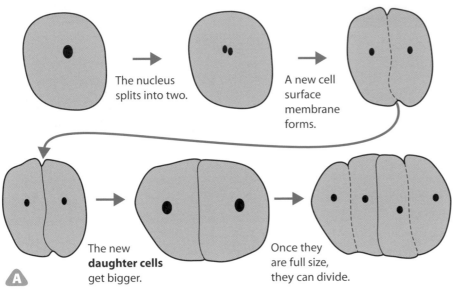

The nucleus splits into two.

A new cell surface membrane forms.

The new **daughter cells** get bigger.

Once they are full size, they can divide.

A

The daughter cells made by cell division are quite small. Before they can divide they need to grow to full size and to do this they require nutrition. Our cells get nutrition from the food we eat. That is why people who do not get enough food may not grow as tall as they should.

3 Look at photo C. 🅗🅢🅦
   a Which cell is dividing?
   b Are these plant or animal cells?
   c How can you tell?
4 a Which life process does cell division help us with?
   b Which life process do muscle cells help us with?

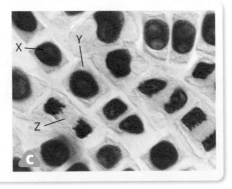

X
Y
Z
C

1 A mnemonic (pronounced '*nem-**on**-ick*') is a silly word or sentence used to remember a list. MRS GREN is a mnemonic to remember the life processes.
   a What does MRS GREN stand for?
   b Think up another mnemonic for the seven life processes.
2 What is cell division?

!

Sometimes cell division goes wrong and cells start dividing faster than they should. Cancer cells do this.

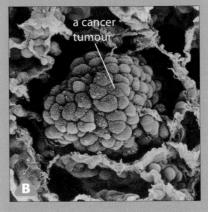

a cancer tumour

B

I CAN...

o explain what happens in cell division.
o recall the seven life processes.

How do cells, tissues and organs work together?

Organs are made from different tissues, and tissues are made of groups of the same cells.

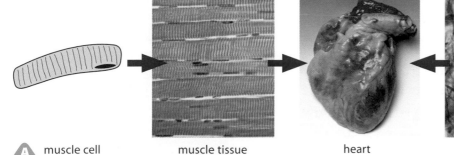

A muscle cell   muscle tissue   heart   nerve tissue   nerve cell

A set of organs working together is called an **organ system**. The heart is part of the **circulatory system**. About 300 heart transplants are carried out each year in the UK, but other parts of the circulatory system are also transplanted to help keep people's hearts working. If blood vessels taking blood to the heart muscle tissue get blocked, these can be replaced using blood vessels taken from the patient's own leg.

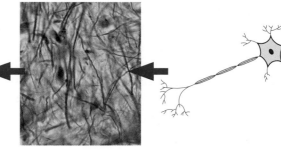

H S W

The circulatory system contains over 100 000 km of blood vessels carrying blood. That's four times around the Earth!

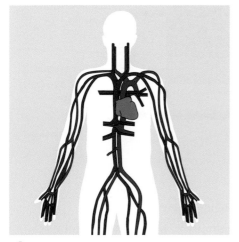

1 What piece of apparatus would be used to show that a tissue contains cells of the same type?   **H S W**

2 What is an organ system?

3 a Name an organ in the circulatory system.
  b What does the circulatory system do?

4 The organs for most transplants are taken from people whose hearts are still beating (although their brains are dead). Why do you think it is important to keep the heart beating?   **H S W**

5 Describe one difference between a heart transplant and transplanting blood vessels?   **H S W**

B The circulatory system contains the heart and the blood vessels. It carries oxygen and food around the body.

There are many other organ systems. Food is broken down in the **digestive system**. The lungs are part of the **breathing system**. The brain is part of the **nervous system**, which carries signals around our bodies.

6 Which life processes do these organ systems help with:
  a digestive system
  b nervous system

I CAN...

o recall that different tissues are grouped together in organs.
o explain what an organ system is.

What is dialysis?

HowScienceWorks

Your kidneys are part of the **excretory system** – a group of organs that excrete (remove) poisonous substances from your body. The substances are taken out of your blood and put into your urine. Some people's kidneys stop working properly. They need to have their blood cleaned by a **dialysis machine**.

The dialysis machine was invented in the 1940s by Willem Kolff (b. 1911). Before that time, people whose kidneys had stopped working died quite quickly.

Your kidneys act like a filter and Kolff's invention uses this idea. In a dialysis machine, a person's blood runs through a tube of a material with tiny holes. Large things, like blood cells, cannot fit through the holes but the poisonous substances are small enough to fit through the holes and so are removed from the blood.

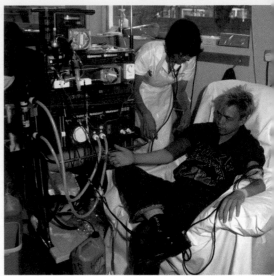

A A dialysis machine.

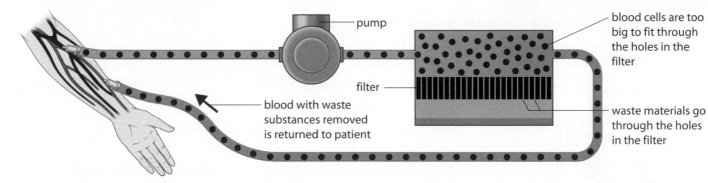

pump

blood cells are too big to fit through the holes in the filter

filter

blood with waste substances removed is returned to patient

waste materials go through the holes in the filter

B How a dialysis machine works.

Today in the UK there are about 18 000 people who need dialysis. Each person spends between 5 and 10 hours, three times a week, connected to a dialysis machine. This is a long time and it would be better if many of these people could get kidney transplants, but there are not enough kidneys to do this.

1 What scientific idea is a dialysis machine based on?
2 How do you think the number of kidneys available for transplants could be increased?
3 Since each person has two kidneys, often a close relative will give a kidney to someone with kidney failure. Some doctors think that people should be allowed to sell their kidneys. What do you think of this idea?

! All of your blood is cleaned by your kidneys every 5 minutes.

How do cells, tissues and organs work together in plants?

Plants have organs that, like animal organs, are made of tissues. Their tissues are made of cells of the same type all working together.

 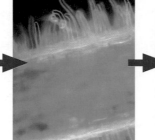  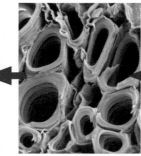 

A root hair cell   root hair tissue   root   xylem tissue   xylem cell

> 1 Name two types of cells found in roots.

Plants also have organ systems. Plants lose a lot of water from their leaves and so need a constant supply from the soil. The roots, stem and leaves form the **water transport system**.

B

Parts of plants are also transplanted. These are called **grafts**. Often the stem of one plant is joined to the roots of another. This is done for a number of reasons. For example, one plant may grow well in a certain soil but a similar plant that looks much better does not grow. Gardeners may graft the stem of the better-looking plant onto the roots of the one that grows well.

> H S W
>
> Plan an investigation to find out which weather conditions make leaves lose water fastest.
> o Which conditions will you try?
> o Which conditions do you predict will cause most water loss?
> o How will you find out how much water has been lost?
> o How will you make it a fair test?

C

2 a What are the organs in a plant's water transport system?
  b Name one tissue you would expect to find in each of these organs.
3 Which is the odd one out and why? root stem leaf flower
4 Draw a diagram to show how you think a graft might be carried out.

> **I CAN...**
>
> o recall the organs in the water transport system in plants.

HowScienceWorks

William is a fish surgeon. It's his job to find out what is wrong with valuable fish and help them to get better. Like a human doctor William needs a very good knowledge of organs. Unlike a human doctor he can't ask the fish how it's feeling!

William needs to do various tests on a sick fish to try to work out what is wrong with it. This might include examining its gills and skin. If he suspects a serious problem he may take a tissue biopsy and look at it under a microscope. In this way he can check for parasites (small creatures that feed on fish) or cancer.

Human doctors perform similar tests and may also take biopsies.

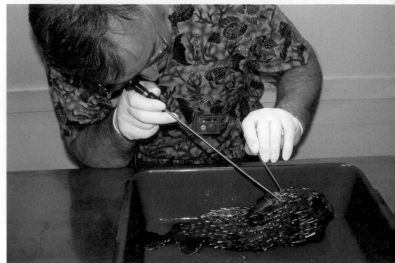

A William examines a porcupine puffer fish. The fish is anaesthetised and can be kept out of water for up to 4 minutes.

The training to be a doctor or fish surgeon involves more study of organs and how they connect with each other in organ systems. There are plenty of fish that a trainee fish surgeon can practice on but it is a bit more difficult for trainee doctors. However, some people ask that, when they die, their bodies are 'left to medical research' which means that student doctors can practice surgery on them to get a better understanding of organs.

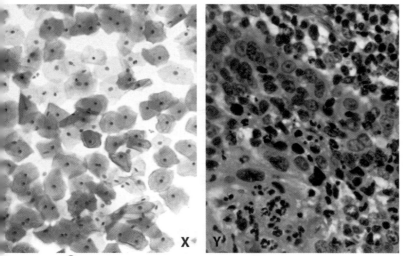

B Doctors also take biopsy samples from humans to check for cancers. Here are two biopsy samples of cells both from a woman's cervix.

HAVE YOUR SAY

Some people think that the bodies of people who have died should always be made available for medical research. What do you think of this idea?

1 List four jobs that need a knowledge of organs and how they work.
2 Look at the biopsy photos.
   a Draw one cell from photograph X and label its parts.
   b In cancer of the cervix the nuclei of the cells are large. Which photograph, X or Y, shows a biopsy from someone with cancer of the cervix?
3 Why don't people who want their bodies left to medical research carry donor cards?

HowScienceWorks

Some animals may soon cease to exist because there are very few left in the world. They are said to be **endangered**. Many zoos have breeding programs, where they try to breed endangered animals and release the young animals back into the wild.

Breeding programs can have problems. Sometimes animals living in zoos do not mate and sometimes their babies die for unknown reasons.

A These scimitar-horned oryx no longer exist in the wild but there is a plan to reintroduce them using animals from breeding programs, such as the one at Cotswold Wildlife Park.

Some scientists have suggested **cloning** some endangered animals to increase their numbers. Cloning does not need a male and a female – just one animal. A cell is taken from the animal, and is used to create a whole new animal. The new animal is an exact copy of the first animal! It's very complicated and expensive to do and does not always work.

B There are less than 300 Sumatran rhinoceroses left in the world. They are also very difficult to breed in zoos.

!

Groups of scientists from all over the world work together at the International Union for the Conservation of Nature and Natural Resources (IUCN) to publish a list of endangered organisms, called the 'Red List'. There are 7725 animals on this list.

1 a What is an endangered animal?
   b How do scientists usually try to help endangered animals?
   c Why does this not always work?

2 Photo C shows Lonesome George. He is the last remaining individual of a certain type of giant tortoise from the Galapagos Islands.
   a How could the numbers of these tortoises be increased?
   b What are the problems with doing this?

3 What do you think the point of the Red List is?

How do animals reproduce sexually?

Just one cell is needed to clone an animal. Normally two cells are needed to produce a new animal in a process called **sexual reproduction**.

These cells are called **sex cells** – male **sperm cells** and female **egg cells**. During **fertilisation** one sperm cell **fuses** (joins) with one egg cell, and the **nuclei** inside them also fuse. This produces a **fertilised egg cell**, which then grows into a new animal.

For fertilisation to happen, the sperm cells must reach the egg cells. **External fertilisation** is when this happens outside the bodies of the animals. This usually occurs in water. In other animals, the male **parent** places the sperm cells inside the female parent. This is called **internal fertilisation**.

1 In animals, what are the male sex cells called?

2 How is a fertilised egg cell formed?

> **!**
> Most animals that use internal fertilisation need to get very close to each other. Not so the paper nautilus. This sea creature (related to squid) detaches its penis, which then swims off by itself to torpedo a female. The male dies soon afterwards.

A Frogs use external fertilisation. The male squirts sperm cells onto the egg cells as the female lays them.

3 Name two animals that use external fertilisation.

4 How do you think scientists find out which animals use which sort of fertilisation?   **H S W**

B These endangered gelada baboons use internal fertilisation.

Old ideas

People did not always know how new animals were made! In Ancient Egypt the River Nile flooded each spring and formed mud pools. These attracted large numbers of frogs. People thought that frogs were produced by mud.

In the same way, until a few hundred years ago many people thought that grain produced mice, that rotting rubbish produced rats and that meat produced maggots.

These sorts of ideas were not scientific. People saw that meat got maggots in it after a while. So they thought that the meat produced maggots, but they did not test this idea.

In 1668, Italian scientist Francesco Redi (1626–1697) had an idea that maggots were caused by flies laying eggs on the meat. He tested this idea by putting meat into a set of jars. He sealed some of the jars, put gauze over the tops of others and left others open. He put all the jars in an area where there were flies. Maggots were only found in the open jars. His **conclusion** was that flies produced the maggots, not the meat.

5 a Why do you think people thought that rotting rubbish produced rats? Ⓗ Ⓢ Ⓦ

 b What experiment would you do to test whether rubbish produced rats? Ⓗ Ⓢ Ⓦ

!

This is a seventeenth century recipe for mice: Place some sweaty underwear in a jar with some wheat. Wait 21 days. The sweat will turn the wheat into mice.

6 Imagine you are journalist in 1668. Write a short article for a newspaper announcing Redi's discovery. Ⓗ Ⓢ Ⓦ

c

Scientific method

Redi used the **scientific method**, which all scientists use today. Scientists think up **theories** (ideas that can be tested) to explain things. Then they do experiments and make **observations** to collect **evidence**. Evidence is any information that can be used to show that a theory is correct or incorrect.

7 Look back at question 4. Ⓗ Ⓢ Ⓦ
 a Rewrite the question using the word 'evidence'.
 b Now answer the question again using the word 'observations'.

I CAN...

o explain what internal and external fertilisation are.
o describe what the scientific method is. Ⓗ Ⓢ Ⓦ

What do the male and female reproductive systems do?

The **reproductive organs** produce sex cells. They form an organ system called the **reproductive system**.

> ! Girls are born with about 100 000 undeveloped egg cells in each ovary.

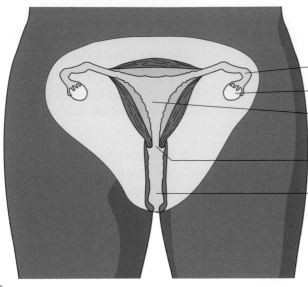
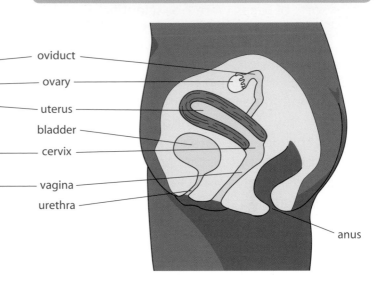

A *The female reproductive system.*

oviduct
ovary
uterus
bladder
cervix
vagina
urethra
anus

In females, the **ovaries** contain small, undeveloped egg cells. Once every 28–32 days, an egg cell from one ovary becomes mature. It is released into the **oviduct** (sometimes called the Fallopian tube or egg tube).

1 a What are the female sex cells called?
  b Where are they released from?

The oviduct is lined with **cilia** that sweep the egg cell towards the **uterus**. The uterus is where the baby will develop. It has strong, muscular walls and a soft lining.

The lower end of the uterus is made of a ring of muscle called the **cervix**. The cervix holds the baby in place during pregnancy. The cervix opens into the **vagina**.

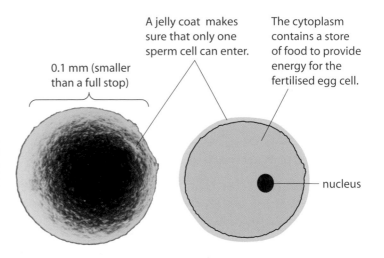

A jelly coat makes sure that only one sperm cell can enter.

The cytoplasm contains a store of food to provide energy for the fertilised egg cell.

0.1 mm (smaller than a full stop)

nucleus

B *A human egg cell is **adapted** to its **function** (job). Magnification ×570.*

2 How does an egg cell get to the uterus?
3 What is the cervix?

Males make sperm cells in their **testes**. The testes are held outside the body in a bag of skin called the **scrotum**. Their position helps to keep the sperm cells at the right temperature to develop properly.

> **!**
>
> Adult men produce up to 100 million sperm cells every day.

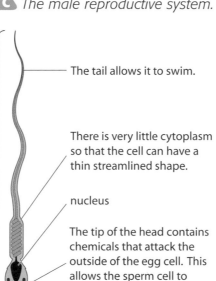

bladder
glands
penis
sperm duct
urethra
testis
foreskin
scrotum
anus

C *The male reproductive system.*

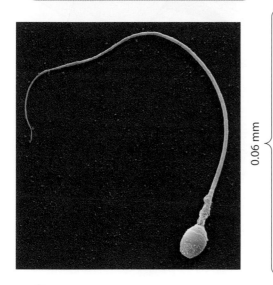

0.06 mm

The tail allows it to swim.

There is very little cytoplasm so that the cell can have a thin streamlined shape.

nucleus

The tip of the head contains chemicals that attack the outside of the egg cell. This allows the sperm cell to burrow inside.

D *A human sperm cell is adapted to its function. Magnification ×4000.*

The penis head is sensitive and is protected by a covering of skin (the **foreskin**). This is sometimes removed, for religious reasons or because it is too tight, in a process called **circumcision**.

After puberty, a man will produce sperm for the rest of his life. A woman's ovaries stop releasing egg cells at about the age of 45–55 – a time known as the **menopause**.

When sperm cells are released from the testes they travel up the **sperm ducts**, where special fluids are added from **glands**. The fluids give the sperm cells energy. Together the sperm cells and the fluids are called **semen**. The semen leaves through the **urethra**. This tube also carries urine from the bladder, but never at the same time as semen.

> **4 a** Where are sperm cells made?
> **b** Do you think sperm cells need to be warmer or colder than the body to develop?
> **5** What is semen?
> **6** What substances can the urethra carry?

7 A woman releases an egg cell every 28 days for 35 years. How many egg cells does she release in total? Show your working.

8 Where does the developing fertilised egg cell get its energy from?

9 Anne's ovaries are not releasing egg cells. Why not? Think of as many reasons as you can.

10 Some women are paid to donate egg cells for scientists to use to find out more about fertilisation. Do you think this is a good idea? Explain your answer.

H S W

> **I CAN...**
>
> o name the parts and jobs of the male and female reproductive systems.
> o explain how sperm and egg cells are adapted to their functions.
> o state that egg cells stop being released in females at the menopause.

How does sexual intercourse result in fertilisation?

Men and women often show that they love each other by having sexual intercourse, also called 'having sex' or 'making love'.

As a man and a woman prepare to have sex, various things happen to their bodies. The woman's vagina becomes moist and the man's penis fills with blood, making it stiff (an **erection**). During sex, the penis is inserted into the vagina and the man moves it backwards and forwards. Eventually semen is pumped out into the top of the vagina. This is called **ejaculation**.

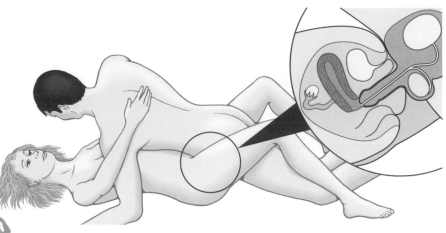

A

1 What fills the penis to make it stiff and erect?
2 What is ejaculation?

The semen is sucked up through the cervix. Small movements of the uterus wall carry it up to the oviducts. Here, the sperm cells start to swim along the oviducts. If a sperm cell meets an egg cell, the sperm cell can burrow into it and fertilise it. In fertilisation, the nucleus of the sperm cell joins with the nucleus of the egg cell. Each nucleus contains half the instructions for a new human and so the baby will have features from both its mother and its father.

3 What is fertilisation?
4 Where does fertilisation occur?
5 Only one sperm cell joins with the egg cell. What do you think happens to all the others?

B *A sperm burrowing into an egg cell (magnification ×4000).*

The fertilised egg cell divides into two. Each of these cells then divides into two again. The cells carry on dividing and form a ball of cells as they travel towards the uterus. In the uterus, the ball of cells (called an **embryo**) sinks into the soft lining. This is called **implantation**. The woman is now **pregnant**.

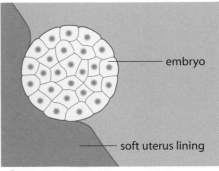

embryo

soft uterus lining

C *Implantation.*

6 What is implantation?
7 Explain why people get features from both of their parents.

Twins

Sometimes, a woman might release two eggs at the same time. If both are fertilised, twins are produced. These twins will not be identical. Sometimes the fertilised egg cell divides in two and the two new cells get separated. Both of these cells can grow into embryos and produce identical twins. Identical twins will either be two girls or two boys. Most animals have more than one baby at a time. Having more than one baby is called a multiple birth.

D *These twins are identical.*

E *These twins are non-identical.*

! Female nine-banded armadillos always give birth to four identical quadruplets.

! Very occasionally, when the fertilised egg cell divides in two, the two new cells start to separate but do not separate fully. In this case the twins will be joined together (conjoined), often at the hip. During World War Two the cruel Nazi 'doctor' Josef Mengele sewed twins together to try to create conjoined twins.

8 a How are non-identical twins produced?
  b How are identical twins produced?
9 a How would you find out how many pairs of identical twins are born each year in the UK? **H S W**
  b Use the method you suggested in part **a** to find out. **H S W**

I CAN...

o describe sexual intercourse and the possible consequences of sex. **H S W**
o explain what happens during fertilisation and where it happens.
o describe how an embryo develops and implants into the uterus lining.

How can science assist fertilisation?

Many couples choose when to have children but some find it difficult to start a family. This may be due to problems with the man's or the woman's reproductive organs. Hospital tests can find out what is wrong.

Damaged or narrow oviducts may stop sperm cells getting to the egg cells. Doctors can try to make them wider. If this does not work, the woman may be given a **sex hormone** to make her produce many egg cells all at once. These are collected and added to the man's sperm cells in a dish. The fertilised egg cells are then implanted in the uterus.

Some men produce very few sperm cells (they have a low **sperm count**). In this case, one sperm cell is taken and injected into an egg cell using a very fine needle.

Helping couples to have a baby in this way is called **IVF** (*in vitro* fertilisation) and the babies are often called **test-tube babies**.

The first successful IVF treatment was carried out in rabbits in 1959. Scientists then did further experiments with mice before they were ready to try IVF out in humans. The world's first test-tube baby, Louise Brown, was born in Oldham in 1978.

IVF is also used in animals today, to increase the numbers of animals that don't breed well in captivity.

> **2** Why do you think scientists tried out IVF on animals before humans? **H S W**
>
> **3** Draw up a list of reasons why IVF is used. Find out if it is used in other situations not mentioned on this page. **H S W**

> **1** Why do you think people like to choose when to have children?

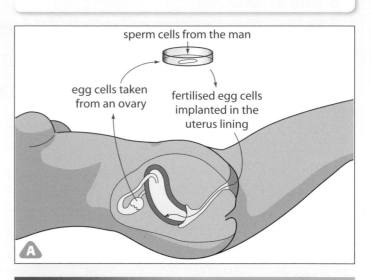

A

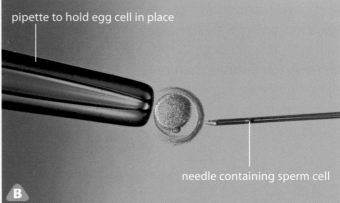

pipette to hold egg cell in place

needle containing sperm cell

B

C *Endangered animals, like giant pandas, are being bred using IVF.*

What happens during the menstrual cycle?

The **menstrual cycle** is a series of events that occur in the female reproductive system. Each cycle takes about a month and is controlled by chemicals called **sex hormones**. These are made in the brain and ovaries.

Menstruation
('having a period')
is when the soft
lining of the uterus
breaks apart. It
passes out of the
vagina along with
a little blood. A
period usually lasts
for 3–7 days.

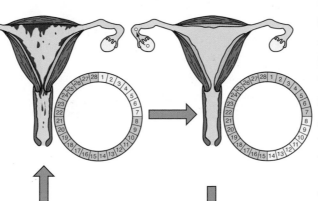

About 14 days after ovulation,
if the egg cell has not been
fertilised, the lining of the uterus
breaks apart again and the cycle
restarts with another period. If
the woman becomes pregnant
the cycle stops.

Periods usually occur once
every 28–32 days, but this
can vary a lot, especially when
periods first start. Sanitary
towels or tampons are used to
absorb the blood.

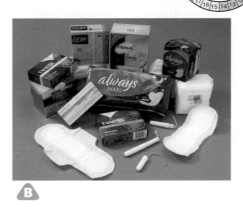

B

3 What happens about 14 days after menstruation starts?
4 Why does the soft uterus lining have to become thick?
5 How might a woman tell that she is pregnant?

1 How long does one complete menstrual cycle take?

Immediately after
menstruation, an egg cell
starts to **mature** in one
of the ovaries. While this
happens, the soft lining of
the uterus starts to build
up again. About 14 days
after the cycle has started,
the egg cell is released.
This is **ovulation**.

The egg cell is swept
along the oviduct towards
the uterus. If the egg cell
meets a sperm cell it can
be fertilised. The soft lining
of the uterus helps to feed
an embryo and the lining
is replaced each cycle to
make sure it can do this.
It continues to thicken for
about a week after ovulation.

2 a What happens during
   menstruation?
  b How long does
   menstruation last?

I CAN...

- explain what happens
  in the menstrual cycle.
- explain the use of some
  sanitary products. **H S W**
- state what ovulation is.

How does the foetus develop during pregnancy?

After an embryo implants into the uterus lining it becomes surrounded by watery **amniotic fluid**, which protects it. The fluid is contained within a bag called the **amnion**.

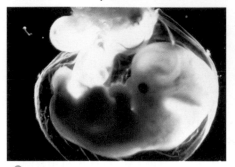

A *At 5 weeks after fertilisation the embryo is about 5 mm long. Its tiny heart pumps blood.*

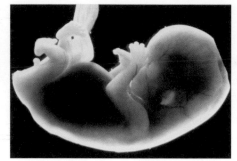

B *When the embryo has developed a full set of organs it is called a* **foetus**. *This takes about 10 weeks, when the foetus is about 4 cm long.*

C *After about 15 weeks the foetus is about 16 cm long. The mother can now feel its movements inside her.*

A **placenta** also grows. This is a plate-shaped organ that is attached to the uterus lining. It provides the developing foetus with the things it needs to grow. Inside the placenta, oxygen, water and food from the mother's blood go into the foetus' blood. Waste materials (like carbon dioxide) go from the foetus' blood into the mother's blood. The **umbilical cord** carries blood between the foetus and the placenta.

The mother's blood does not mix with the foetus' blood. This is because the mother's blood is pumped around her body under a lot of pressure, which would damage the delicate foetus.

1 What protects the developing embryo?
2 After how many weeks can the mother feel the baby move?

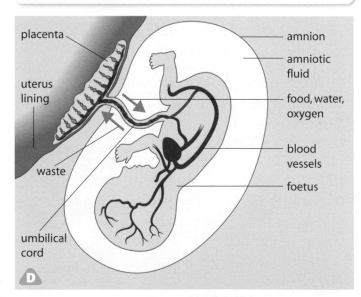

D

3 What is the job of:
   a the placenta   b the umbilical cord?
4 a What does the foetus take from the mother's blood?
   b What does the foetus give to the mother's blood?
5 The lungs do not work in a foetus. Why do you think this is?
6 Why does the foetus' blood not mix with the mother's?

I CAN...

o describe how a foetus is protected and cared for in the uterus.

How can a mother care for the developing foetus?

It is important that a pregnant woman eats a healthy diet since she must provide the foetus with food, including vitamins and minerals.

She also needs to take regular exercise to keep her muscles strong and her circulatory system working well. **Ante-natal classes** teach women special exercises to prepare them for birth. Most pregnant women go for **ultrasound scans**. These make pictures of the foetus that doctors use to see if there are any problems.

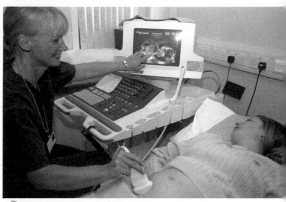

A *A woman having a scan.*

1 Suggest some changes that occur in a woman during pregnancy.
2 Why is exercise important during pregnancy?

Some viruses, alcohol, drugs and chemicals from cigarette smoke will all go through the placenta and into the foetus, where they can cause damage.

Viruses are tiny microbes that can cause diseases. The virus that causes rubella can cause a foetus to become deformed. Girls should be vaccinated against rubella.

Too much alcohol will damage a foetus' brain. Illegal drugs, like heroin, also cause brain damage in the foetus. Doctors need to be very careful about what medicines they give to pregnant women.

> **!** Sadly, sometimes drugs that are given to help pregnant women actually damage the foetus. In the 1950s, a drug called thalidomide caused many babies to be born with very short arms and legs.

3 What is a premature baby?
4 What things should a mother avoid during pregnancy? Explain your answer.
5 Ultrasound scans were introduced in the 1950s. What effects do you think they have had? List as many as you can. **H S W**

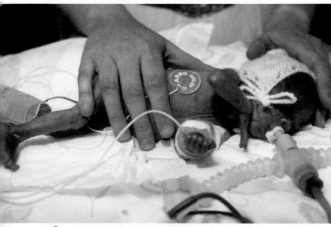

B *A premature baby.*

The blood of a woman who smokes carries less oxygen than it should, which means that the foetus may not get enough oxygen. A baby that has not received enough oxygen is likely to be **premature** (born small and early).

I CAN...

o explain why doctors encourage pregnant women to eat good diets and avoid harmful substances. **H S W**

What happens during and just after birth?

The **gestation period** is the time from fertilisation until birth. In humans this is about 9 months (40 weeks). When the baby is ready to be born, the uterus begins to contract (push) and this is the start of **labour**. The **contractions** start gently but become more powerful. The muscles of the cervix then slowly relax, making it wider. At some stage, the amnion breaks and the amniotic fluid flows out of the vagina.

> ! The American opossum has a gestation period of about 12 days. The gestation period for an African bush elephant lasts for about 22 months.

Once the cervix is about 10 cm wide, the strong contractions of the uterus push the baby through it, usually head-first. This can be very painful, and the woman may be given medicine to stop some of the pain.

The umbilical cord is then tied and cut. The scar from the umbilical cord is the **navel** (belly button).

> **2** Write captions for photos B and C to say what is happening.

Within half an hour after the birth, the placenta breaks away from the uterus and passes out through the vagina. This is called the **afterbirth** and marks the end of labour.

In the first few months, the baby needs to be fed on milk. The breasts contain **mammary glands** that produce milk. This milk contains nutrients to give the baby energy and help it grow. It also contains **antibodies** – substances that help to prevent diseases caused by microbes. After a few months the baby can eat semi-solid food.

> **3** How does a young baby get its food? Explain in as much detail as you can.
>
> **4** How do you think modern medicine has made giving birth easier? H S W

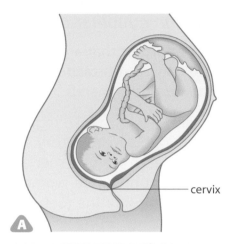

A — cervix

> **1 a** What happens to the cervix during labour?
> **b** Why does this happen?

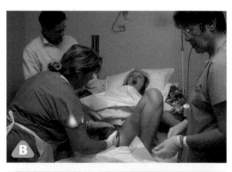

B

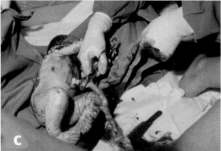

C

> ### I CAN...
> - state how long the human gestation period is.
> - recall how a baby is born and cared for.

7Be Growing up

What are puberty and adolescence?

Babies become toddlers at about 12 months. Toddlers become children at about 3 years old. Between the ages of 10 and 15, big physical changes start to happen in children's bodies, including fast growth. This period of time is called **puberty** and is usually finished by the age of 18. Girls generally start puberty before boys.

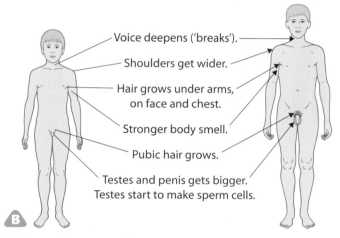

- Voice deepens ('breaks').
- Shoulders get wider.
- Hair grows under arms, on face and chest.
- Stronger body smell.
- Pubic hair grows.
- Testes and penis gets bigger. Testes start to make sperm cells.

B

- Stronger body smell.
- Underarm hair grows.
- Breasts develop.
- Ovaries start to release eggs.
- Hips get wider.
- Pubic hair grows.

A

Puberty is started by sex hormones, which are chemicals released by the ovaries and testes.

> **! H S W**
>
> Until the mid-nineteenth century, choirboys sometimes had their testes cut off (castration) before reaching puberty. This stopped their voices 'breaking' and they grew up to be singers called castratos. The last one was Alessandro Moreschi (1858–1922).

C

4 What is adolescence?
5 What do we mean by 'emotional changes'?
6 Why do you think choirboys are no longer castrated? **H S W**

> **!**
>
> Dogs go through puberty at around 10 to 14 months – and they can get acne too!

1 a What is puberty?
 b What chemicals control puberty?
 c Where are these chemicals produced in girls and boys?
2 Make a list of the physical changes that happen to both boys and girls.
3 Imagine you write a magazine advice column. Somebody tells you about their terrible acne. What advice would you give?

Sex hormones also cause spots (**acne**) and emotional changes, including boys and girls becoming more interested in each other. The time when all these emotional and physical changes occur is called **adolescence**.

I CAN...

- recall what happens in adolescence.
- explain why these changes happen and when they happen.

7Be Lifecycles

The series of changes in an organism as it gets older is called a **lifecycle**.

Animals with long lifecycles, like humans, usually only have a few babies at a time. This is because the babies are protected by growing inside the mothers (**internal development**) and the adults take good care of the babies after they are born. A long lifecycle also means that the **offspring** need a long time before they can reproduce.

Animals with short lifecycles produce many more offspring because they often don't protect them, and so many of the offspring will die. But it does not take long for the offspring to be able to reproduce.

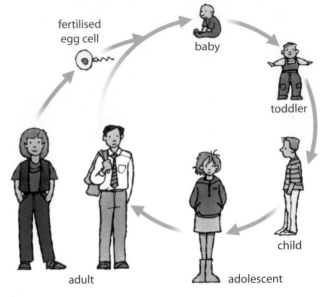

fertilised egg cell

baby

toddler

child

adolescent

adult

A The human lifecycle.

When scientists try to help endangered species they often need to help with fertilisation and with looking after the offspring. In animals with long lifecycles, they take very good care of both the mother and her offspring.

B The agile frog was only found in one pond on the island of Jersey. Females lay thousands of eggs but most die or are eaten by ducks. So, scientists took eggs from the pond and cared for them. Then they put the small frogs back into the wild to grow and reproduce.

C This Sumatran orangutan was kidnapped by a rival female. He was rescued, fed and given back to his mother.

1 a In animals that use internal development, where do their foetuses grow?
  b What do you think is meant by **external development**?
  c Give an example of an animal that uses external development.

2 Draw a copy of the human lifecycle (without the pictures). Label the time taken between each stage.

3 Make a list of the ways in which science can help:
  a endangered animals to increase their numbers
  b couples to have babies.

HAVE YOUR SAY

Some people think we should get rid of zoos and only care for endangered species in the wild. What do you think about this?

How**S**cience**W**orks

About 180000 new homes are built in the UK each year. These take up a lot of room and mean that there is less room for animals and plants to live.

A Oakdale Housing Estate in Wales.

B Ecologist Colin Plant.

Colin Plant is an **ecologist** – a scientist who studies organisms and the areas where they live. Colin is often asked by developers to study areas where houses are to be built. He writes a report to describe what would happen to the plants and animals if the houses were built.

Sometimes, rare organisms are found in an area. This can mean that the development is not allowed to go ahead or the development is delayed. The development might be delayed so that:

• the rare organisms can be moved to another area
• the development can be redesigned to allow the organisms to continue to live there; this is known as **sustainable** development.

If something is sustainable it means that it allows things to continue into the future.

C The building of this tourist centre on Drumkinnon Bay was stopped for two weeks so as not to disturb the breeding of rare powan fish.

1 a In order to build in some places it is the law that a survey is done of the organisms living there. Do you think this is a good law or not? Explain your reasons.
  b Who should carry out this survey?

2 What problems might building a city the size of London cause for the UK? Think of as many problems as you can.

3 What is a sustainable development?

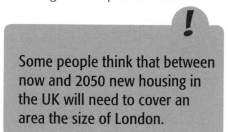

!

Some people think that between now and 2050 new housing in the UK will need to cover an area the size of London.

What is in a habitat?

The place where an organism lives is called a **habitat**.

A *Woodland habitat.*

B *Pond habitat.*

C *Desert habitat.*
meerkats

D *Arctic habitat.*

E *Underground habitat.*

1 **a** Imagine you went to each of the habitats A–E. Predict two organisms that you would expect to find in each. Ⓗ Ⓢ Ⓦ
  b How would you test your predictions? Ⓗ Ⓢ Ⓦ

The word **environment** is used to describe the conditions in a habitat. Most of the conditions are caused by **physical environmental factors**. Examples include how much light there is, how wet it is, how much wind there is and how hot it is. These factors can all be changed if buildings are constructed in an area.

An ecologist often uses a **quadrat** – a square frame that is thrown around the habitat. The number of plants of one type that are inside the frame are counted for each throw. Knowing how many plants are inside a few quadrats helps you to work out the number of the plants in the whole area.

An environmental factor (e.g. the amount of light) can also be measured in each quadrat throw. This will allow you to make links between environmental factors and where certain plants grow best. It also helps you to see exactly where each type of plant is found in the habitat – its **distribution**.

F *Using a quadrat.*

2 Describe the environment in each of the habitats A–E.

3 Describe your environment at the moment.

4 Suggest what pieces of equipment you would need to measure the different environmental factors. Ⓗ Ⓢ Ⓦ

5 How could the amount of light in an area be affected by a new building? Ⓗ Ⓢ Ⓦ

Ⓗ Ⓢ Ⓦ
How would you investigate why different numbers of a plant grow in different areas of a habitat?
o How would you measure the environmental factor?
o How would you survey the plants?

Organisms are **adapted** to live in their habitats. This means that they have features and behaviours that allow them to survive in an area. For example, fish have gills and fins, which are **adaptations** for living in water. Their fins will not let them walk on land and their gills will not let them breathe air. Fish are not adapted to living on land.

Behaviour describes what an animal does. Animals are born with some behaviours (e.g. fish can swim, human babies cry). However some behaviours are learned (e.g. fish learn where to find food, human babies learn to walk).

All the animals and plants that live in a habitat make up a **community**. Members of communities may have similar adaptations to cope with the problems of living in a particular habitat. For example, many organisms that live in fast-flowing rivers have adaptations to stop them being swept away.

Some organisms only live in certain small areas of a habitat. Centipedes live in woodland but are usually only found under logs and leaves. Smaller areas where things live are called **microhabitats**.

G

6 How are ducks adapted to:
  a swimming on water
  b flying?

!

Your body is a habitat and head lice live in a microhabitat – human hair! They suck blood from people's scalps.

H

7 Which of these are physical environmental factors?
  light frog wind bush ant fungus temperature bird

8 Photograph I is of a hogsucker fish.

flexible, streamlined body

sucker to attach to rocks

I

  a What habitat do you think it lives in? Explain your answer.
  b Draw a plant that might live in the same habitat. Label its adaptations. It does not have to be a real plant!

9 Describe the distribution of human head lice.

10 a List the two types of behaviour.
   b Give the name of an animal and describe how its behaviour helps it to survive.

I CAN...

o describe the environments of some habitats.
o give some examples of how organisms are adapted to their habitats.
o explain what a distribution and a community are.
o use a quadrat to work out distributions of plants. H S W

How are organisms adapted to where they live?

Great crested newts are adapted to living in and around ponds. They are protected by law. It is illegal to catch or harm them or to disturb their habitats.

dark colour for camouflage – it's difficult to spot them underwater

wide feet to stop it sinking into mud on land

powerful, wide tail for swimming

The newt has a thin skin that allows it to take in oxygen from the water. However, the skin must be kept damp, even out of water.

A *Great crested newts are adapted to living in and around ponds.*

1 What adaptation do great crested newts have for swimming?

2 Why do you think they are protected by law? **H S W**

In 2004 the Joseph Rowntree Foundation wanted to build 540 homes near York. However, some great crested newts were found on the site. The development may have caused the newts to die out because their adaptations only allow them to survive in areas with ponds. The plans were changed to include bigger and better ponds for the newts, so that their numbers could increase. The plans were approved in 2007.

Pond plants are also adapted to where they live. Photo B shows some duckweed.

3 Why might putting up houses without any ponds cause the newts to disappear?

4 A representative wrote this in a local newspaper: '… the Joseph Rowntree Foundation will continue to progress its interest… in a sustainable way'. In what way is the development sustainable? **H S W**

Duckweed floats so that the leaves get plenty of sunlight for photosynthesis.

B *Duckweed is adapted to living in ponds.*

How would you find out whether duckweed plants are only adapted to live in fresh water or whether they can live in salty water too?

o How much salt would you use? (There are 30g of salt in every litre of sea water.)

o What would you look for in the duckweed plants?

5 How do duckweed plants get a lot of sunlight?

Vultures live in the desert. They urinate on their legs to keep cool! The urine evaporates which cools them down.

dried urine

C

It's not just buildings that cause problems for habitats. Most scientists think that humans are making the Earth warm up (**global warming**) and that this is causing problems in many habitats – including places where very few humans live, like the Arctic.

Polar bears are adapted to hunting seals, which live on the ice. Warmer temperatures in the Arctic mean that there is less ice and so fewer places to hunt seals.

6 How are polar bears adapted to the cold in the Arctic?

7 Ecologists in Canada have found that polar bears are 10% thinner than they were 20 years ago. Suggest a reason for this. Ⓗ Ⓢ Ⓦ

If the Earth continues to warm up, some species that are adapted to desert habitats may spread into new areas.

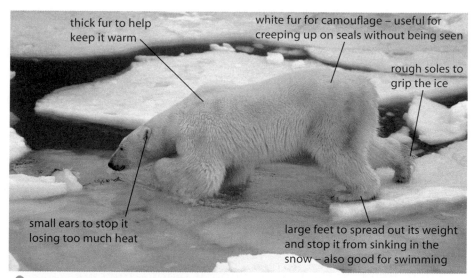

thick fur to help keep it warm

white fur for camouflage – useful for creeping up on seals without being seen

rough soles to grip the ice

small ears to stop it losing too much heat

large feet to spread out its weight and stop it from sinking in the snow – also good for swimming

D Polar bears are adapted to living in the Arctic.

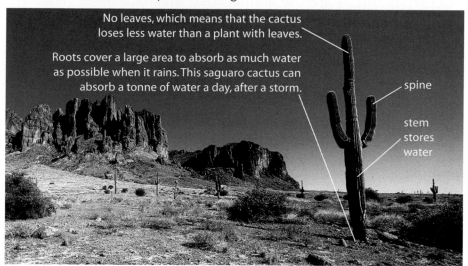

No leaves, which means that the cactus loses less water than a plant with leaves.

Roots cover a large area to absorb as much water as possible when it rains. This saguaro cactus can absorb a tonne of water a day, after a storm.

spine

stem stores water

E Cacti are adapted to living in deserts. They may soon grow in new areas that have become warmer and drier due to global warming.

8 a A cactus has spines on its stem. Why do you think these are useful?

b Most cacti grow very slowly. Suggest why this is.

9 Photo F shows a jack rabbit.

a Suggest what habitat it is adapted to.

b Suggest some reasons for its long ears.

large ears to allow heat to escape and improve hearing

does not drink and gets all its water from its food

large hind legs to run away quickly (at up to 70 km/h) from animals that might eat it

F

I CAN...

- state some adaptations of plants and animals for different habitats.
- explain why changes in habitats cause problems for organisms.
- give reasons why the plans for a development may need to be changed.

How are organisms adapted to natural environmental changes?

There are natural, regular changes that occur in habitats. Changes during a day are known as **daily changes**, and changes during a year are called **seasonal changes**. Organisms are adapted to these changes.

Daily changes

Many flowers give off a smell to attract the animals that pollinate them. Some flowers open at night – they are **nocturnal** and so are the animals that pollinate them. The flowers shut during the day to avoid wasting scent when the animals are not around.

> **2** Daisy flowers open during the day and shut at night. Explain why.

Many animals are born with behaviours that change as daily changes occur. Great crested newts are nocturnal so that they are less likely to be seen and eaten. However, other animals, like many owls, are also nocturnal so that they can catch and eat other nocturnal animals! These animals have adaptations for darkness; newts have excellent eyesight and owls have superb eyesight and hearing.

Seashore organisms are adapted to tides. Sea anemones use tentacles to feed underwater. When the tide goes out, they pull in their tentacles to stop them drying out.

> **1** Describe how the amount of light in a wood changes during:
> **a** a day
> **b** a year.

A *Saguaro cacti flowers only open at night when the bats that pollinate them are active.*

!

A barn owl can hear a mouse's heartbeat from 10 metres away.

Ⓗ Ⓢ Ⓦ

How would you find out if water fleas are found in different places during the day and at night?

D

B *A sea anemone under water.*

C *A sea anemone when the tide is out.*

Seasonal changes

In winter, **deciduous** trees lose their leaves because there is not much light for photosynthesis and their leaves lose water (which cannot be replaced if it is frozen in the ground). **Evergreen** trees have tougher leaves that don't lose much water, and so they keep their leaves all year round. These trees can grow quite far north where the summers are short. By keeping their leaves, they can start photosynthesising and growing again as soon as there is enough liquid water and light.

Some plants, like poppies, die completely in the winter. Their **seeds** grow into new plants in the spring. In other plants, like bluebells, only the parts above ground die. They leave **bulbs** underground that will grow again in the spring.

E   evergreen trees   deciduous tree

3 a In which season was photograph E taken?
  b How do you know this?

Animals are also adapted to survive in winter. Many animals, like rabbits, grow longer fur to help keep them warm. The ptarmigan has brown feathers in summer and white ones in winter. It also grows feathers on its feet in the winter that act like snow shoes.

ptarmigan

F

G

4 Why do you think the ptarmigan's feathers change to white in winter?

An animal's behaviour can change too. In the autumn squirrels collect and store nuts to eat during the winter. Some animals eat a lot in the autumn and sleep through winter. This is **hibernation**. Great crested newts hibernate and so do hedgehogs, dormice, frogs and ladybirds.

Some birds fly to warmer places during the winter where there is more food. This is called **migration**. Swallows migrate to South Africa in October and come back to the UK in April.

!

An Arctic tern flies about 35 000 km each year as it migrates from the Arctic to the Antarctic and back again.

5 Why do animals that hibernate eat a lot in the autumn?

6 a How do these physical environmental factors change from summer to winter in the UK?
    i light   **ii** temperature   **iii** rain
  b Suggest how you could collect measurements to show how one of these factors changes.   Ⓗ Ⓢ Ⓦ

7 How are these organisms adapted to survive the winter in the UK?
  a hedgehog   **b** oak tree   **c** swallow   **d** poppy

I CAN...

o give examples of adaptations to daily and seasonal changes.

o give examples of animals that hibernate, migrate and are nocturnal.

o state some differences between deciduous and evergreen trees.

7Cd Finding food

How are animals adapted to feeding?

Predators are animals that hunt other animals. The animals that they hunt are their **prey**. Predators have adaptations that allow them to catch their prey. The predators in the pictures are from Africa and live in an open grassland habitat (called savanna).

> **1 a** What is a predator?
> **b** Name one predator from the African savanna.
> **c** Name one predator that you might find in the school grounds.

forward-facing eyes to spot prey

hooked beak acts like a pair of scissors to cut flesh

huge, sharp claws (talons) to catch hold of prey

A *A Lanner falcon.*

sandy-coloured fur helps to camouflage it

forward-facing eyes to spot prey

powerful legs to help it run fast

large, sharp teeth to rip at flesh

sharp claws to grab prey

B *A lion.*

Animals that are prey have adaptations to help them avoid being eaten.

> **2 a** List two adaptations that predators have in common.
> **b** How does each adaptation help the predator to trap its prey?
> **3 a** List two adaptations that prey have in common.
> **b** How does each adaptation help the animal avoid predators?

eyes on the side of its head so it can see behind

large horns for protection

large ears to listen for danger

sandy-coloured hair for camouflage

long legs to make it tall and help it to see danger

C *An oryx.*

sandy-coloured fur for camouflage

large ears to hear danger

eyes on the side of its head so it can see behind

powerful hind legs to help it run fast

D *A scrub hare.*

Animals that eat other animals are called **carnivores**. They use senses like sight, smell and hearing to find their prey. Animals that eat plants are called **herbivores**. They use senses like sight and smell to find plants to eat.

> **4** Humans have senses. Which senses do we use to find food?

Woodlice are **decomposers**. They eat rotting wood and leaves. How would you investigate what behaviour woodlice have for finding food?

○ Think about the conditions in which rotting wood and leaves are found.

○ You could use a **choice chamber**. The compartments can be filled with different substances.

○ Calcium chloride removes moisture from the air but can harm woodlice if it touches them.

Many animals also have special adaptations for eating. For example, birds have different shaped beaks depending on what they eat.

F *Oyster catchers have long beaks to search in sand for shellfish.*

G *Ducks have flat beaks to sift out weed and small snails from water.*

H *Swallows have short, pointed beaks to catch insects in the air.*

I *Finches have thick, strong beaks to crush seeds.*

5 How is a Lanner falcon's beak adapted for eating other birds?

6 a What is a herbivore?
  b List all the herbivores on these two pages.

7 a What is a carnivore?
  b List all the carnivores on these two pages.

8 Look back at page 40.
  a What is a nocturnal animal?
  b Name one predator that is nocturnal.
  c What sense does this animal use to hunt?
  d What is this animal's prey?

9 a Many shellfish are found deep in the sand along beaches. Shelducks are ducks that live along the sea shore. Explain why shelducks don't eat shellfish buried in sand.
  b Suggest what shelducks eat.

!

The pistol shrimp stuns its prey with a loud noise that it makes with its claws.

I CAN...

○ describe some ways in which predators and prey are adapted to finding food and feeding.

What problems can parasites cause?

A **parasite** is an organism that lives in or on another living organism (called its **host**).

Some parasites cause diseases and even death. One-celled organisms called trypanosomes (found in Africa) live in blood and cause a disease called sleeping sickness. About 100 people die every day from this disease.

Discovery

Using a microscope Sir David Bruce (1855–1931) discovered trypanosomes in the blood of cattle that had sleeping sickness. He injected blood from sick animals into animals that had no trypanosomes. Those animals then got the disease and had trypanosomes in their blood. His later investigations showed that trypanosomes caused human sleeping sickness and were carried between animals by blood-sucking tsetse flies.

Controlling the disease

One way to control the disease is to decrease the numbers of tsetse flies. This can be done by:
- using poisons
- using traps
- destroying the flies' habitat (areas with bushes and small trees)
- killing wild animals that trypanosomes can live in
- releasing sterile males.

In this last method lots of specially bred male tsetse flies are given a dose of radioactivity. This makes them 'sterile' which means they cannot pass working sperm onto the females when they mate. It works because the females only mate once.

HowScienceWorks

1 Head lice are parasites. What are their hosts?

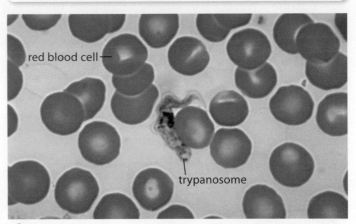

red blood cell

trypanosome

A *Trypanosomes (magnification × 500).*

B *The black part of this trap contains a bottle of cow urine. Tsetse flies are attracted towards the bottle, fall into it and die.*

2 For each method of controlling sleeping sickness, explain:
  a how it works   **b** what problems it might cause.
3 What was Bruce's evidence for sleeping sickness being caused by trypanosomes?
4 Suggest a way of controlling sleeping sickness that does not affect tsetse flies.

What are food chains and food webs?

Every organism contains a store of **chemical energy**. Animals eat things to get this store of chemical energy. A **food chain** is a way of showing what eats what in a habitat. The arrows show the direction in which energy travels.

In this food chain you can see that oryx eat grass and lions eat oryx. Chemical energy is passed from the grass to the oryx and then from the oryx to the lion.

Food chains always start with organisms that make their own food. These are called **producers**. Plants are producers. Animals are **consumers**, which means that they have to eat other things. A food chain ends with a **top predator**.

grass   is eaten by   an oryx   is eaten by   a lion

This can be written as a food chain:

grass ——————→ oryx ——————→ lion

A *A food chain.*

> **1** Look at the food chain and name:
> **a** two consumers **b** a predator
> **c** a producer   **d** a top predator.

On the African savanna it is not only oryx that eat grass. Many other animals do too. To show this we need to use a **food web**. A food web can also show how some animals (called **omnivores**) eat both plants and other animals.

> **2** Look at the food web.
> **a** What eats grass?
> **b** What do caracals eat?
> **c** Write down one of the two longest food chains in the food web.
> **d** Write a list of the organisms in your food chain from part **c**. Describe what each one is by writing one or more of these words next to it: carnivore consumer herbivore omnivore producer top predator
> **3** Why are plants called producers?

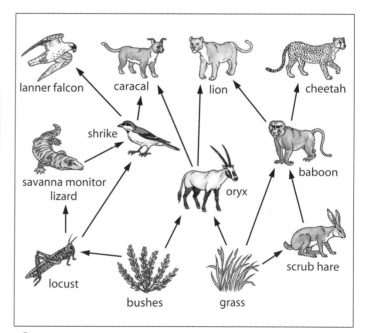

B *A food web.*

I CAN...
- draw and explain food chains and food webs. **H S W**
- recall the words that describe organisms in a food chain (e.g. producer, predator).

How can we tell what eats what?

When ecologists study a habitat they try to find out what organisms live there and how they feed. They can then use this information to construct food webs.

Pooters and **sweepnets** are often used to collect organisms from a habitat. In woods, ecologists can also shake tree branches and collect the organisms that fall from them. This is called **tree beating**.

A *Using a pooter.*

1 a Where would you use a sweepnet? Ⓗ Ⓢ Ⓦ
  b You would not use a sweepnet to collect animals from dead leaves. Why not? Ⓗ Ⓢ Ⓦ
  c What would you use to collect animals from dead leaves? Ⓗ Ⓢ Ⓦ
2 If you remove any animals from a habitat to look at, you should always replace them where they were found. Suggest why.

B *Using a sweepnet.*

Where an animal is found may give an ecologist an idea of what it eats. For example, aphids are found on plant stems because they feed on juice inside the plant. Ladybirds are found near aphids because they eat aphids.

aphids

C

3 Look at photos D and E. Ⓗ Ⓢ Ⓦ
  a What do you think woodlice feed on? Give a reason for your answer.
  b What do you think will eat the fly? Give a reason for your answer.

D

E

An ecologist can also find evidence from animal waste.

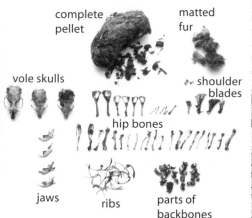

F *Thrushes are small birds that drop snails on stones to break their shells. The stones are called thrush anvils.*

complete pellet
matted fur
vole skulls
shoulder blades
hip bones
jaws
ribs
parts of backbones

G *Owls swallow their food whole and then cough up the bits that cannot be digested. The coughed up bits come out as a pellet.*

H *This dropping contains the seeds of what the bird has eaten.*

Animal droppings are distinctive shapes and can be used to show what animals are in a habitat and what they eat. Identifying the animal droppings found near a damaged plant or a dead animal will provide evidence for what animal was responsible.

Other evidence includes teeth marks, footprints and distinctive trails. For example, snails leave trails of slime behind, which can often be seen around damaged plants.

Once an ecologist has put together a food web, you can see how the organisms in a habitat rely on each other for food (**feeding relationships**). You can also see how they **compete** with each other. For example, earthworms are eaten by hedgehogs and shrews. The hedgehogs *and* shrews are in **competition** with each other for the worms.

Humans also compete with plants and animals. When building projects take place we compete for space.

4 Name one animal that an owl eats. **H S W**

5 a What do thrushes eat? **H S W**
   b How would you find evidence to support this? **H S W**

I *An ecologist working in the savanna in Africa would know that this hyaena has been killed by a lion because of what the teeth marks look like.*

6 Name two ways of finding out what a bird eats. **H S W**

7 Teeth marks are often found on the bark of trees. Suggest how you would go about finding out what animal made the marks. **H S W**

8 Look at the food web on page 45. Which animals compete for baboons?

9 Plants also compete with each other. Suggest what they compete for.

I CAN...

○ plan how to find evidence of what eats what in a habitat. **H S W**

○ use information to work out which organisms are in competition with each other. **H S W**

Ecologists are often called in to look at habitats before changes are made. Changes include planned building work or plans to kill certain animals that are causing a problem.

A
rabbit droppings

HowScienceWorks

A farmer has called in an ecologist to advise on what might happen if he kills the field mice in his wheat fields. The farmer wants to know what affect this might have on other organisms in the fields. The ecologist has been to the field and done a study. The photographs show the evidence collected.

B
stoat   rabbit

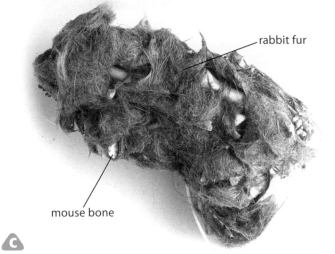

C
rabbit fur
mouse bone

D   E

1 Why do you think the farmer wants to kill the mice?
2 Use the photographs to draw a food web for the field.
3 For each of the animals in the food web:
   a describe an adaptation for surviving in this habitat
   b explain how this adaptation helps it to survive.
4 Write a letter to the farmer to explain what effect the removal of the field mice might have on this habitat. Use your food web to help you.

How Science Works

Many things are sorted into groups to make our lives easier. In a supermarket similar foods are grouped together. Signposts show where the grouped foods are (e.g. frozen foods). The grouped foods are then displayed in smaller groups (e.g. the ice creams are all together).

> 1 a Why are foods grouped together in a supermarket?
>   b How would you find fizzy orange in a supermarket?

Large libraries use Dewey Decimal Classification. Books are divided into 10 numbered categories (000, 100, 200 … 900). Science books are in category 500. The categories are split, according to their types, into smaller categories. *Exploring Science* is a textbook, so is in category 507. In the library you need to look up the Dewey number of the book in an index, but then finding the book is easy.

A

B *These library books are sorted into groups using Dewey Decimal Classification.*

> **!** Dewey Decimal Classification was invented in 1876 by a librarian called Melvil Dewey. He was a great fan of simplifying English spellings and is the reason that Americans spell catalogue as 'catalog'.

> 2 a Describe how things are organised in your kitchen at home.
>   b How is this different to the organisation of a supermarket?
>   c Why are the things organised like this?
> 3 a A menu featuring Melvil Dewey's spelling system contains the following: Masht potato, Butr, Steamd rys, Letis, and Ys cream. Write these items out in standard UK spelling.
>   b There are similar arguments about the spelling of scientific words, for example sulphur/sulfur and foetus/fetus. Do you think we should try to simplify spellings or leave spellings as they are? Explain your thinking.

What is variation?

Books and foods are sorted into groups using similarities and differences. Scientists use the same ideas to sort **organisms** into groups. Differences between organisms are known as **variation**. There is a lot of variation between different types of animals.

C *A fox.*

A *An aye-aye.*

B *A ground squirrel.*

1 Draw a table to show at least two similarities and two differences between the animals shown in photos A, B and C. **H S W**

There is less variation between animals of the same type. Organisms of the same type are said to belong to the same **species**. For example, humans all belong to the same species. A species is a group of organisms that can reproduce with one another to produce **offspring** that are also able to reproduce.

2 Write a list of five things that may be different between different people.
3 Describe the variation between:
   a zebras   b potatoes in a supermarket.

Horses and donkeys can reproduce with each other. Their offspring are called mules. However, mules cannot reproduce. This means that horses and donkeys must be different species.

D *These zebras are all one species but there is variation between them.*

Horses and zebras can reproduce with each other. They produce zebroids. Zebroids cannot reproduce. Animals like this are called hybrids and usually only occur when animals are in captivity.

E

4 What is a species?
5 Tigers and lions can reproduce to give 'ligers'. Ligers cannot reproduce. What does this tell you about lions and tigers?

Correlations

Some differences are linked. For example, people with blond hair usually have blue eyes. These links are called **relationships** or **correlations**. Relationships are best seen using line graphs or bar charts. Bar charts are used when one of the things you are looking at has a limited set of options, for example eye colour, where there are either brown or blue eyes but nothing in between. We also use bar charts when looking at numbers that are grouped together.

Chart F shows a strong correlation between having blond hair and blue eyes because many people fall into this category. There is no relationship between having blond hair and brown eyes because there are only a few people in this category.

Graph G shows the relationship between the heights of oak trees and their masses. Line graphs are used when the numbers you measure are a range of values that change gradually. The relationship is that 'taller trees have larger masses'.

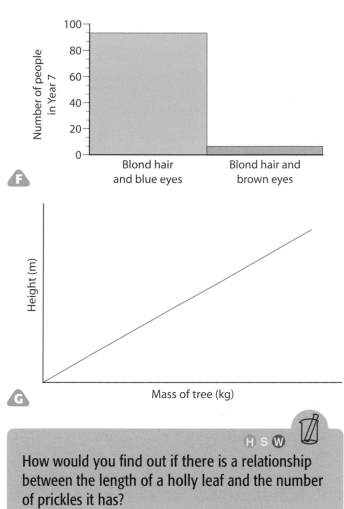

F

G

H S W

How would you find out if there is a relationship between the length of a holly leaf and the number of prickles it has?

6 What relationship does line graph H show? **H S W**

7 Look at pictures I and J. Write down two things that are: **H S W**
   a the same in each species
   b different in each species.

H

I

J

I CAN...

o recall what a species is.
o describe some examples of variation between different species and between members of the same species.
o identify correlations or relationships from bar charts and line graphs. **H S W**

What are continuous and discontinuous variations? HowScienceWorks

If you measure the height of people in your class, you will find that there is a range of heights. Very few people will be exactly the same height.

This variation is described as **continuous**. There is a range of values that change gradually.

A

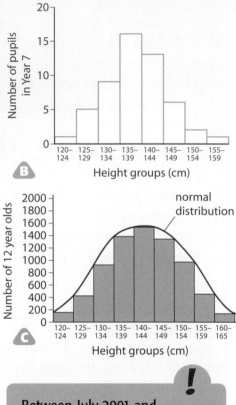

B

C

normal distribution

You can see that chart B is almost shaped like a bell. A lot of pupils have an average height and fewer pupils fall into the groups on either side.

The more pupils we measure, the more like a bell the chart becomes. Chart C shows the data for several thousand 12 year olds. This bell shape is known as **normal distribution**. It is called 'normal' because this is what we expect to find in things that show continuous variation.

If you choose a small **sample** size you may not get a bell-shaped bar chart. This is because you might choose a small group of people who are particularly tall or short. Taking larger sample sizes is always much better for getting more reliable results.

Some people can roll their tongues and others cannot. This variation is described as being **discontinuous**. This means that there is not a continuous range of options.

Between July 2001 and February 2002 over 1.5 million measurements were taken from over 11 000 people in the UK National Sizing Survey. The data was used by shops to design clothes that fitted people better.

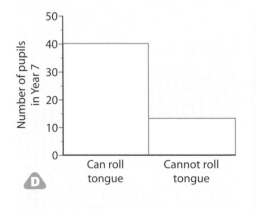

D

1 a Copy the list of features below and say whether each variation is continuous or discontinuous.

natural eye colour	having a scar
natural hair colour	having a cold
having a tattoo	naturally curly hair
length of hair	having pierced ears

  b Which of these would you expect to show normal distribution?

2 a Explain why the National Sizing Survey measured so many people.

  b What measurements do you think they took?

  c What relationships do you think they looked for in the data?

What is inherited variation?

Children share features with their mothers and fathers but do not look exactly like either parent. They vary.

1 **a** The man in photo D has a son. Which of the photos do you think shows his son? Explain your reasoning.
   b Which of the photos do you think shows the man's mother? Explain your reasoning.

Brothers and sisters also share some features but often look very different from each other.

Half of the information needed to make a child comes from the mother and half from the father. So, children have features from both parents but the exact mixture of features in each child will be different.

We **inherit** features from our parents. The variation caused by inheriting features is called **inherited variation**. Natural eye colour, ear shape and dimpled chins are examples.

2 Name three features that can be inherited.
3 What percentage of the information needed to make a child comes from the mother?
4 Nicola's mother has blue eyes and blond hair. Her father has brown eyes and blond hair. Both Nicola and her sister have brown eyes and blond hair.
   a Which feature of her parents has not been passed on to either Nicola or her sister?
   b Nicola has a scar on her leg. Do you think this is an example of inherited variation? Explain your reasoning.

I CAN...
o say how inherited variation is caused.
o identify examples of inherited variation. **H S W**

How can the environment cause variation?

The inherited features of the plants and animals we eat give them their taste. But the taste can also be affected by the surroundings in which the plants or animals grew.

An organism's surroundings are called its **environment**. In all environments there are things that can change the organism. These are called **environmental factors** and include things like rainfall, sunshine, chemicals and the amount of space things have in which to live.

Some people think that **organic** and **free-range** foods taste better or are healthier. Organic products are grown without using harmful chemicals. Free-range animals have lots of room in which to move.

Variation caused by environmental factors is called **environmental variation**. The way that free-range chickens look compared with caged hens is an example.

1 a What does the word 'environment' mean?

b Which environmental factor is different between where normal potatoes and organic potatoes are grown?

B *These free-range chickens produce eggs.*

C *These caged chickens also produce eggs.*

2 a Some people think that free-range chicken tastes better than chicken from caged hens. What is this taste an example of?

b Describe one difference between the environments of the chickens in photos B and C.

c Describe one environmental variation between the two chickens.

3 For each sentence write down the environmental factor and the environmental variation it causes.

a Bill finds the cress seedlings that he grew in a dark cupboard are yellow.

b Jayesh discovers small insects on an apple tree. The tree has holes in its leaves.

c Rose puts fertiliser on her sunflower plant and it is now 2 m tall.

Hydrangea flowers are affected by the acidity of the soil. In acidic soils they are blue and in alkaline or neutral soils they are pink.

D

Algae are tiny, green organisms found in pond water. They are not plants but, like plants, they need light for photosynthesis. Fertilisers help plants to grow. How would you find out if fertilisers also help algae to grow?

o Which fertilisers would you choose?
o How would you measure how much the algae had or had not grown?

E

Humans also have environmental variations. Having a scar is an example. Something has happened to produce a scar. Long hair is another example. In this case the environmental factor is fashion!

Photos F, G and H show environmental variations. However, many features are caused by both environmental and inherited factors (e.g. our heights).

4 How have environmental factors affected you, either now or in the past? Make a list of five examples.

F

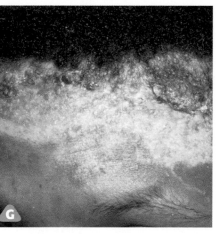

G

H

5 Look at photo F. What environmental variation does the apple on the right show?

6 The person in photo G has been in an accident involving a fire.
   a What is the environmental factor that has affected him?
   b What environmental variation has been caused?

7 What environmental factor do you think has shaped the tree in photo H?

8 Look at photo D. What sort of soil is the hydrangea growing in?

9 Copy the list of features below. For each feature, say whether it is an example of inherited variation, environmental variation or both.
   natural eye colour   natural hair colour   a scar   having a cold
   naturally curly hair   length of hair   a tattoo   small nose
   being good at roller-blading   speaking French

Learned **behaviours** are also examples of environmental variation. You are born with the ability to make sounds but the language you speak is learned from those around you.

I CAN...

o explain what environmental variation is.
o identify examples of environmental factors that cause environmental variation. Ⓗ Ⓢ Ⓦ

7Dc Describing differences

How can we describe and group organisms?

Whenever you read a description of a plant or animal you are reading about variation. Passage A is from a book about nature by a Roman called Pliny the Elder (23–79 CE). Writings like this provide evidence for the animals that were known about in ancient times.

1 a What animal do you think is being described in passage A? This is difficult!
  b How does this passage provide evidence that Romans travelled widely?

There are two other animals that look rather like camels. One of these ... has a neck like a horse's, feet and legs like an ox's, a head like a camel's. It is a reddish colour and covered with white spots. For this reason it has been called the cameleopard.

A

Descriptions of organisms differ depending on the audience they are written for. Sometimes a writer wants to create a certain impression. Sometimes a writer only wants to give factual information.

The _____ started on toward the place from where the call surely came, then returned to him [Buck], sniffing noses and making actions as though to encourage him. But Buck turned about and started slowly on the back track. For the better part of an hour the wild brother ran by his side, whining softly. Then he sat down, pointed his nose upward, and howled.

B *A passage from a novel called* Call of the Wild *by Jack London (1876–1916).*

Imperiously he leaps, he neighs, he bounds.
And now his woven girths he breaks asunder;
The bearing earth with his hard hoof he wounds;
Whose hollow womb resounds like heaven's thunder;
The iron bit he crusheth 'tween his teeth,
Controlling what he was controllèd with.

C *A verse from a poem called* Venus and Adonis *by William Shakespeare (1564–1616).*

Wood White
This delicate example has a much more dainty flight pattern than the related Small White. It is reluctant to settle in warm weather.
Wingspan: about 40 mm
Wing colour: mainly white with greyish smudges. Males have black tips on forewings.

D *An extract from* Field Guide to Insects of Europe.

2 In passage B Buck is a dog. The missing word is the name of an animal. What do you think the missing word is?
3 a Look at passage C. What animal do you think Shakespeare was describing?
  b What impression was Shakespeare creating about this animal?
4 Look at passage D. What sort of insect do you think is being described?

The parts of the Wood White that are being described are its wings. A description of an animal's parts can help us to identify its name. However, for the description to make sense we need to know what the parts are called.

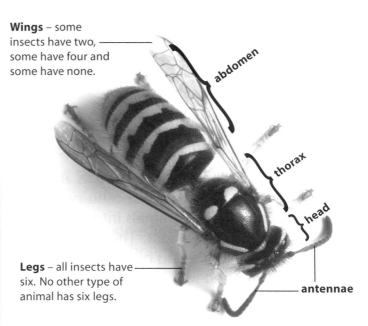

Wings – some insects have two, some have four and some have none.

abdomen

thorax

head

Legs – all insects have six. No other type of animal has six legs.

antennae

5 a What are the names of the sections in an insect's body?
  b Which section of an insect's body are the wings attached to?
  c You find a new animal. How could you tell that it is an insect? Choose from the following:
  it has two wings   it is black and yellow
  it has six legs   it has antennae

 The parts of an insect. Insect bodies have three sections.

Arachnids are another type of small animal. They have eight legs. We can put insects and arachnids into different groups based on the number of legs they have. Putting things into groups like this is called **classification**. These groups can then be used to help work out what a newly discovered organism is.

All sorts of things are classified, including foods in supermarkets and even fingerprint patterns. There is a great deal of variation in fingerprints. Everyone has a different set of fingerprints that do not change. However, fingerprints do have some common features and so can be classified. Scenes of crime officers look for fingerprints and compare any that they find with a chart showing the different types.

F

There are three main types of fingerprint pattern. Along with others in your class, how would you try to find out what these three main types are?
o Design a chart to be used by scenes of crime officers.

H S W

G Compare this fingerprint with yours and see how much they vary.

H S W

The modern way of classifying fingerprints was developed in 1888 by the British scientist Sir Francis Galton (1822–1911). Fingerprints were first used for criminal investigations in the UK in 1901.

6 What is the proper name for grouping things together?
7 Fingerprints found at the scene of a crime cannot prove that a person committed a crime. What can they prove?   H S W

I CAN...

o classify organisms into groups based on variations in their features.   H S W

HowScienceWorks

There is enormous variety in our lives. To make finding things and identifying things easier we put similar things together into groups. This is called classification. Different things are classified in different ways.

> Items in supermarkets are first sorted into groups depending on how the items need to be stored. The items are labelled with common names.

> Books in libraries are first sorted into categories depending on what they are about. The books are given coded numbers.

> Scientists sort organisms into groups depending on what they look like. We give the organisms Latin names.

A

B

C

! New species are still being discovered. This lemur was discovered in Madagascar in 2005.

D *Goodman's mouse lemur* (Microcebus lehilahytsara).

Organisms are classified according to what they look like but only their inherited variations are considered (not environmental variations).

Some scientists think that Linnaeus' system needs to be updated. Some want to group the five kingdoms into three 'domains' depending on what the insides of the cells look like. Others want to classify organisms depending on the organisms that they were descended from, thousands of years ago.

HAVE YOUR SAY

Do you think the system of classifying organisms should be changed?

1 Look at the branching diagram on page 59. Draw out a similar diagram, adding in all the different groups of invertebrates.

2 When a new organism is found, scientists need to classify it. Explain why it is better to find several of the new organisms before deciding which group to put the organism into.

Acids in action

Acids are a very useful group of chemicals. Just over 150 years ago Justus von Liebig suggested there was a link between the wealth of a country and the amount of acid that it used.

He said this because sulphuric acid was used in a number of important manufacturing processes. Today, acids are still used to make fertilisers, paints and plastics. You can also find acids in foods and drinks.

Many acids are dangerous and need to be handled with care. When using chemicals, we need to have a **risk assessment**. This tells us how dangerous a chemical is. It also suggests how we can use the chemical more safely, for example by wearing gloves or using only small amounts.

> We may judge the commercial prosperity of a nation from the amount of sulphuric acid it consumes.

A *Justus von Liebig (1803–1873).*

B *Part of the job of a health and safety officer is to carry out risk assessments. This makes sure that the factory runs safely and that the risks to the workers and the local community are kept to a minimum.*

1 Name three products that are made using acids.

2 What is a risk assessment?

3 Suggest two precautions that you might take when handling a dangerous acid.

4 You could test von Liebig's idea by doing a survey to collect data and showing it on a graph.
 a What data would you need to collect?
 b How would you present your graph?
 c What would this graph look like if his prediction were still true today?

5 Think of a plus, a minus, and an interesting point about this statement:
 The UK should use less acid.

In the red

How can we tell if something is an acid?

Gardeners need to know if soil is acidic or not, to know which are the right plants to grow in that type of soil. They might test the soil using a meter like the one in photo A. Before this technology was invented, gardeners often used products from the plants themselves to tell them whether something was an acid.

Some plant colours will change when they mix with acids. A dye which can change colour is called an **indicator**. One example is **litmus**. This can be red or blue, or sometimes purple (blue and red together). You can also get litmus paper, which changes colour in the same way.

A Gardeners often test the soil for acidity.

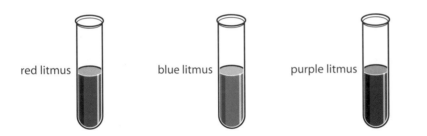

red litmus   blue litmus   purple litmus

B The colours of litmus.

Acids always turn litmus red, so you can test a substance with litmus to see if it is an acid or not. If the litmus stays purple, or turns blue, then it is not an acid. Other indicators include blackberry juice and tea.

H S W

How could you see if red cabbage works as an indicator?
- What would you do to the leaves to get the colour out?
- How could you separate the coloured juice from the leaves?

C

1 Name three indicators.
2 Predict the colour of purple litmus when mixed with:
    a sulphuric acid   **b** tap water   **c** lemon juice.   **H S W**
3 A few drops of litmus solution were added to some toothpaste. The litmus turned blue. What does this tell you about toothpaste? **H S W**
4 Sally crushed up some purple berries from a bush, and mixed them with a little water. When she mixed the juice with some wet washing powder, it changed colour to red.   **H S W**
    a Is the berry juice acting as an indicator? Explain your answer.
    b Which of these best describes the wet washing powder?
      A definitely an acid   B definitely not an acid   C possibly an acid
      Explain your answer.

I CAN...

- give some examples of substances that can be used as indicators.
- test for acids using litmus.   **H S W**

What is an alkali?

In ancient times, Arabic scientists took ashes from fires and mixed them with water. This liquid was boiled with animal fats to make the first soap. In Arabic, the ashes were called 'al qali'. We use the word 'alkali' to describe a group of substances that feel soapy. However, many alkalis are too dangerous to feel. This is because they can start to attack the natural oils in your skin. Your skin can start to turn into soap!

In some ways, alkalis are the opposite of acids. They make indicators go a different colour. Alkalis turn litmus blue. Many substances are neither acids nor alkalis. These are called **neutral**. Pure water, and salt and sugar solutions are all neutral. Neutral substances do not change the colour of litmus.

A *Ashes from a fire contain alkalis.*

How could you use this colour chart for litmus to find out if something is an acid, an alkali or neutral?

o What apparatus would you use?

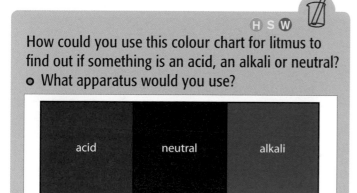

| acid | neutral | alkali |

B

C

Oven cleaners often contain alkalis. The grease in the oven is attacked by the cleaner, and turns into soap. This helps the cleaning process. Note the hazard symbols, which show people how to stay safe.

1 An indicator called methyl orange turns red in acid, and yellow in alkali.
   a What colour would this indicator turn with grapefruit juice? **H S W**
   b What colour would it turn with oven cleaner? **H S W**
2 What is a 'neutral' substance?
3 State whether these substances are acid, alkali or neutral:
   a vinegar   b water   c salt   d lemon juice   e sugar   f soap

I CAN...

o test for alkalis using litmus.   **H S W**
o describe how some alkalis are dangerous.

How can we measure the strength of acids?

Some acids are stronger than others. A simple indicator like litmus can show us whether something is an acid, an alkali or neutral. However, it cannot tell us whether an acid or alkali is strong or weak.

It is always more precise if we can measure something rather than just describe it. In 1909 Søren Peter Sørensen (1868–1969), a Danish chemist, was working to control the quality of beer manufacture. He designed the **pH scale** as a way of measuring how acidic the beer was.

We can measure pH using a pH meter or **universal indicators**. A universal indicator is a mixture of indicators that gives a range of different colours, depending on the strength of the acid or alkali. It comes as a liquid or as test papers. It gives the same range of colours as a rainbow: red, orange, yellow, green, blue and purple. We can use it to measure the pH on a scale which runs from 1 to 14.

1 a What is universal indicator?
b What is it used for?

2 a What pH number would a substance have if it turned universal indicator orange?
b Would it be an acid or an alkali?
c Would it be strong or weak?

strong acid			weak acid			neutral	weak alkali			strong alkali			
1	2	3	4	5	6	7	8	9	10	11	12	13	14

A The pH scale.

Your skin is naturally slightly acidic; it has a pH of about 5.5. Most soaps are alkaline, with a pH of about 9 or 10. Some people find that using soap can dry out their skin and so some manufacturers have now developed alternatives that match the pH of skin. Most shampoos and shower gels are slightly acidic, though they may not all match the pH of skin precisely.

3 What colour would a soap with a pH of 5.5 turn universal indicator?

B Some products match the pH of your skin.

How could you find out the pHs of different skin products?
o What apparatus would you need?

H S W

This means that the substance attacks and damages things including skin and eyes.

This means that the substance can make your skin blister or become itchy.

pH
14 —
13 — oven cleaner
12 —
11 —
10 — washing powder
9 — toothpaste / indigestion powders
8 —
7 — blood / pure water
6 — milk / skin
5 —
4 — fizzy drinks
3 — vinegar
2 — lemon juice / stomach acid
1 —
0 —

C *The pH of some common substances.*

Checking the pH is also important in the environment. We need to keep a check on air and water quality. The pH of the air and the water is checked regularly to make sure that it falls within safe limits. This is particularly important near to factories which produce acids. Pollution from them can cause acid rain, or harm wildlife in the local rivers.

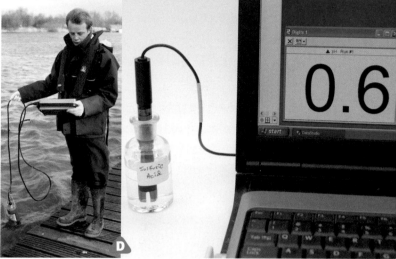

D

4 What is the pH of:
   a stomach acid   b pure water   c skin   d soap?

5 Copy and complete table E.

Name of chemical	Colour of universal indicator	Acid, alkali or neutral	pH
hydrochloric acid		strong acid	
			7
sodium hydroxide	purple		
carbon dioxide solution		weak acid	

E

6 Find out about the use of acids and alkalis in one of these situations:
   a hair and skin care   b stings and bites   Ⓗ Ⓢ Ⓦ
   c treatment of soil   d preserving food.   Ⓗ Ⓢ Ⓦ

7 A sample of water taken from a river near a sulphuric acid factory showed a pH of 5.   Ⓗ Ⓢ Ⓦ
   a Is this acid, alkali or neutral?
   b Do you think this represents a pollution problem? Explain your answer.
   c What extra evidence might you need to collect before coming to a conclusion?

I CAN...

o describe how the strengths of acids and alkalis can be measured on the pH scale.
o give some examples of the pH values of common substances.
o explain the importance of environmental checks on pH levels. Ⓗ Ⓢ Ⓦ

What is an acid?

Scientists look for patterns in the way that things behave. They use observations to sort things into groups based on their properties. Acids have these properties:

• they can be corrosive
• they have a sharp taste
• they can make indicators change colour.

One of the first scientists to group substances into acids and alkalis was Robert Boyle, who lived in the seventeenth century. His book, '*The Sceptical Chymist*', published in 1663, said that scientists should always ask questions and not just take things on trust. A **theory** is a way of explaining why things behave in the way that they do. Boyle suggested that all theories should be tested by experiment. The results of the experiments would provide **evidence**, which could support the theory, or suggest that it was wrong.

As knowledge about acids increased, scientists tried to come up with a rule to decide which substances were acids. In about 1800, one theory was that all acids contained oxygen. It was difficult to test this theory at first because scientists were not sure about what all the different acids contained. Today we know all the substances that make up acids. Some examples are shown in table B.

HowScienceWorks

A *Robert Boyle (1627–1691).*

1 State three properties of acids.
2 Who was the first scientist to suggest grouping substances into acids and alkalis?
3 a What is a theory?
   b What do scientists do to test whether a theory is correct?

Name of acid	What it contains
sulphuric acid	hydrogen oxygen sulphur
nitric acid	hydrogen nitrogen oxygen
phosphoric acid	hydrogen oxygen phosphorus
ethanoic acid	carbon hydrogen oxygen

B

4 How many of the acids in table B contain:
   a sulphur   b oxygen?
5 Explain whether the evidence from table B supports the idea that acids contain oxygen.
6 What other theory would also fit this evidence?
7 Hydrochloric acid contains hydrogen and chlorine. How does this evidence help us to decide between the two theories?

Now we believe that all acids contain hydrogen. This is a true statement, but it is not enough to decide whether something is an acid. Some substances which contain hydrogen are not acids, such as petrol, alcohol and water. Alkalis such as sodium hydroxide and potassium hydroxide also contain hydrogen.

A better way of defining acids is to say that they contain hydrogen that is given off in bubbles when the acids are added to metals. Photo C shows that only the acids form bubbles with the magnesium ribbon. The other two liquids contain hydrogen but do not form bubbles. As scientists have learned more about chemicals, they have come up with newer theories about acids that have improved on earlier ideas.

| hydrochloric acid | ethanoic acid | water | alcohol (ethanol) |

C *Magnesium will bubble when you put it into acids.*

8 The 'p' in pH stands for '*potenz*' – the Danish word for power or strength. What do you think the 'H' stands for?

9 Name:
  a an acid that contains hydrogen and oxygen
  b an acid that does not contain oxygen
  c a substance that contains hydrogen that is not an acid.

10 Look at photo C.
  a Which is the stronger acid – hydrochloric or ethanoic?
  b What is the evidence for this?

11 Sherelle said, 'I've seen an experiment where they dropped potassium metal into water and it fizzed and caught fire. That means that water must be an acid'.
  a Do you agree with Sherelle's statement? Give reasons based on the evidence.
  b What does this hazard symbol mean?
  c Why might it appear on containers of potassium?

D

I CAN...

- state that all acids contain hydrogen.
- describe some of the evidence to support this theory.
- describe how theories change when new evidence is found.

What happens when an acid is added to an alkali?

A Insect stings can be very painful.

A bee sting is acidic. It has a pH of about 3.5. To stop a bee sting hurting you can add a weak alkali. The alkali will **neutralise** the acid. The pH of the affected area will become closer to 7. Wasp stings are alkaline – about pH 10. They need to be neutralised with a weak acid.

1 a What is the pH of a bee sting?
  b Is this acidic, alkaline or neutral?
2 Bicarbonate of soda solution has a pH of about 9. Why is this a good thing to treat a bee sting with?
3 a What type of substance would you use to treat a wasp sting?
  b If someone was in your kitchen and got stung by a wasp, suggest something that you could find in your food cupboard to put on the sting to relieve the pain.

When an acid and an alkali are mixed, they attack each other and turn into new substances. We say that a **chemical reaction** has occurred. The reaction of an acid with an alkali is called **neutralisation**. If exactly the right amounts of acid and alkali are mixed, you will end up with a neutral solution. The change in pH during neutralisation can be measured using universal indicator or a pH meter. Beaker X in photo B contains sodium hydroxide solution, with a few drops of universal indicator solution. Each time the acid is added, you can measure the pH.

B Neutralising an alkali with an acid.

4 a What is the colour of the universal indicator in beaker X? Ⓗ Ⓢ Ⓦ
  b What pH is the sodium hydroxide solution? Ⓗ Ⓢ Ⓦ
5 Look at beaker Y. Ⓗ Ⓢ Ⓦ
  a How can you tell that just enough acid has been added to neutralise the sodium hydroxide?
  b What is the pH?
6 a Look at beaker Z. Does the beaker contain more acid or more alkali? Ⓗ Ⓢ Ⓦ
  b How can you tell?
  c What is the pH?

Another way of changing the pH of an acid or alkali is by diluting it. If you add more water, the pH will get closer to 7. If there is an acid spill, safety officers will try to deal with it by diluting it if possible. This is usually safer and easier than neutralisation with an alkali.

Our bodies use neutralisation reactions to keep the blood and our digestive systems at a constant pH. The hydrochloric acid in your stomach has a pH of 1 or 2. This acid helps to break down your food. If you produce too much acid, you may suffer from indigestion, or heartburn. Remedies like Milk of Magnesia® are called **antacids**. They contain alkalis to cancel out some of the acid and help keep the balance right. The alkalis are weak (usually about pH 9), so that they do not make your stomach too alkaline. Toothpastes also contain a weak alkali to reduce the acidity in your mouth.

C *The person in the lime green safety suit has been dealing with a spill of hydrochloric acid from a tanker crash. A co-worker dilutes the acid on his suit with water to make it safe to take the suit off.*

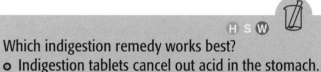

Which indigestion remedy works best?
o Indigestion tablets cancel out acid in the stomach. How could you find out which indigestion tablets are best?

D *Make sure that you carry out a simple risk assessment to keep risks down.*

7 Why would it not be a good idea to use a solution of sodium hydroxide (pH 13) to neutralise any excess acid in your stomach? **H S W**

8 a Concentrated sulphuric acid is too dangerous for you to use. How is the sulphuric acid made safer so that you can use it? **H S W**

b When sulphuric acid dissolves in water, it gives off heat. Safety advice says: **Always add the concentrated acid slowly to cold water when diluting. Never the reverse.** Why do you think it is safer to dilute the acid this way round? **H S W**

I CAN...

o explain what a neutralisation reaction is.
o describe some examples of neutralisation reactions.
o explain how diluting an acid or an alkali will bring the pH closer to 7.

Where do chemical factories get built?

Several hundred years ago, when the first large factories were built, the factory owners built houses for the workers nearby, so that they could all walk to work. Any pollution from the factory affected the people who lived in the area.

We are now much more aware of health and safety issues. Factories tend to be built in industrial zones, well away from where people live. Even so, local residents often raise objections when a new factory is proposed. They may be concerned about the increase in traffic or possible problems with pollution. These objections have to be considered by the local council or the government before the plans for the factory are approved.

B A modern industrial chemical complex.

HowScienceWorks

A Campaigners often oppose the building of new factories.

A factory making sulphuric acid will often be near the sea, so that the raw materials can be brought in by ship. It is also important to have good links by rail and road, so that the tankers carrying the products can get to the customers easily. Building new factories can bring jobs and wealth to an area. Councillors and ministers need to balance the risks against the benefits before coming to a final decision.

1 a How has the way people get to work changed in the last 100 years?
b Why is this?
c How has this changed where factories are built?

2 State two factors that will be taken into account when deciding where to place a new chemical factory.

HAVE YOUR SAY

Imagine that there is a plan to build a sulphuric acid factory near where you live. What do you think of this idea? Write a letter to the local newspaper or your MP setting out reasoned arguments for or against the idea of building a new factory locally.

A **chemical reaction** occurs when chemicals join or break apart to form new chemicals. Chemical reactions are happening all around us. Sometimes it is obvious that there is a reaction taking place. In a firework display, you can see the colours and the smoke, and hear the bangs.

A *Fireworks are chemical reactions.*

The chemicals inside a glow-stick react together to give off light energy. The reaction lasts for several hours. When all the chemicals have been used up, the light fades. Some reactions are less obvious, like when the dough in a bread roll rises or when bread and burgers are cooked.

B *Glow-sticks.*

Not all chemical reactions are useful. On 16 May, 1968 a gas explosion caused this block of flats in London to collapse, killing four people. Now, gas is rarely used in tower blocks. Electric cookers and heaters are used instead.

C

1 a Give three examples of chemical reactions.
  b Are these reactions useful, harmful, or both?
2 What observations tell you that a chemical reaction has taken place when:
  a fireworks go off
  b you cook a burger?
3 In a petrol station, you will often see a notice telling you not to smoke and to switch off mobile phones. Why do they give this safety advice?
4 'There are more useful reactions than harmful ones.' Do you agree with this statement? Give some examples to support your case.

Why do some reactions keep going?

Some reactions occur when two chemicals are mixed. Other reactions need energy to make them happen (e.g. cooking food, splitting water using electricity).

When you cook food, the heat from the cooker causes chemical changes in the foods. If you turn the heat off, the food stops cooking. The chemical reactions stop.

A Chemical reactions started by heat change raw foods into cooked foods.

B Lighting a firework.

A third type of reaction needs energy to start it off, but it will then keep on reacting on its own. A firework has to be heated to get it started. The blue touch paper is lit with a match and then you have to step away. There is enough heat from the burning paper to start the firework off. Once the firework is alight, you don't have to add any more heat. The firework will keep burning until all the chemicals have been used up.

1 Look at photo A. How can you tell that a chemical reaction has happened when the eggs and the onions are cooked?

2 a What type of energy is used to start the reaction in photo B?

  b How do you supply the energy to light a match?

C The fireworks in this display were set off using electrical detonators.

With a big display, it would be too dangerous and too difficult to light the fireworks individually with a flame. Electrical **detonators** are used to start these fireworks off.

When a substance burns, it reacts with the oxygen in the air. You have to put a little energy into the substance to split it up and start the reaction. When it reacts with oxygen to form products, a lot more energy is given off. We notice this extra energy as heat, light and sometimes sound.

Air is about 20% oxygen. A burning splint placed into a gas jar of pure oxygen will burn more fiercely. If you blow the splint out so that it is just glowing, oxygen will make it burst into flames again. This is the test for pure oxygen.

3 Name two types of energy that can be used to start a reaction off.
4 Name three types of energy that can be given out in a chemical reaction.
5 Look at photo D. How could a burning splint be used to tell if a gas were oxygen or carbon dioxide?

D A glowing splint put into a jar of oxygen.

Metals that are used in fireworks will burn in oxygen with a particular colour to form **oxides**. For example, magnesium burns with a white flame to make magnesium oxide. We can write down what happens in a **word equation**:

magnesium + oxygen ⟶ magnesium oxide
reactants   product

6 How can you tell that a new substance is formed when magnesium burns from: Ⓗ Ⓢ Ⓦ
  a photo E
  b the word equation?
7 Sparklers contain iron. Ⓗ Ⓢ Ⓦ
  a Write a word equation for the reaction that takes place when a sparkler is lit.
  b Use ideas about energy and chemical reactions to explain what happens from the time that you light the sparkler until it goes out.

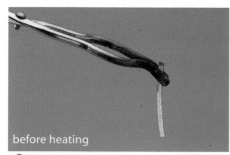

before heating

E This magnesium will burn and form a white ash when heated.

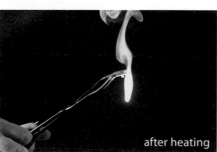

after heating

F You can see the white ash on the tongs.

Heating the magnesium starts the reaction off by turning some of it into a gas. The magnesium then reacts with the oxygen, making magnesium oxide. During the reaction lots of energy is given out. There is enough heat energy to keep the reaction going and there is a surplus which is given off as heat and light.

Ⓗ Ⓢ Ⓦ

How do fireworks get their colours? Liquids containing metals can change the colour of a Bunsen flame.
o How would you find out which metal produces which colour?

I CAN...

o explain how some reactions need energy to get them started.
o write word equations for reactions of metals with oxygen. Ⓗ Ⓢ Ⓦ
o test for oxygen gas. Ⓗ Ⓢ Ⓦ

7Fd Fire safety

How do you put out a fire?

For a fire to burn, three things are needed:
- a substance that burns (the fuel)
- energy to start the fire (usually heat)
- oxygen (usually from the air).

These things are shown in the **fire triangle**. To put out a fire, you need to take away one of the three sides of the fire triangle. **Fire extinguishers** work by cooling the fire, or by stopping oxygen getting to the fuel.

A The fire triangle.

B The safety team on standby at this firework display are ready to put out any fires.

There are different types of fire extinguisher. It is important to choose the right one for each type of fire. Using the wrong type of extinguisher may be dangerous and can even make the fire spread.

Extinguisher type	Type of fire used on
water	wood, paper, cloth
carbon dioxide	electrical fires
foam (AFFF)	wood, paper, petrol, solvents, paints, plastics
dry powder	fires involving metals or electrical fires

C Different types of fire extinguisher.

Water is often used to put out fires because it takes away the heat. However, water should never be used when oil is burning. The water sinks through the oil, and the heat turns the water into steam. The steam rises very quickly to the surface of the oil, pushing the burning oil out of the way and making the fire spread out. The best way to put out a petrol or oil fire is to cover it (e.g. with sand, earth or a fire blanket) to keep the oxygen away.

A chip pan fire … **D**

… with water added! **E**

1 What are the three things needed for a fire to burn?
2 Which side of the triangle is taken away if you put out a fire with:
   a water   b a fire blanket?

Water should never be used on an electrical fire as you may get a serious electric shock. The electricity should be turned off at the mains, and a dry fire extinguisher used. This smothers the flames by covering them in a fine layer of powder or carbon dioxide gas, which cuts off the oxygen supply.

F *Foam can be sprayed onto a plane to stop oxygen reaching the fuel. The wet foam also helps to cool the fire.*

3 The burger van at the fairground has a fire blanket and a carbon dioxide extinguisher. Explain why these types of extinguisher are needed there. Ⓗ Ⓢ Ⓦ

4 Explain why you should never put water onto:
   a an oil fire **b** an electrical fire. Ⓗ Ⓢ Ⓦ

A forest fire is too big to put out using normal extinguishers. It can be very difficult to stop it spreading. Forests often have wide gaps between some of the trees, called fire breaks, which stop the fire from spreading any further.

! Fires can naturally break out in forest areas. These often start during very dry weather. People who look after the forest let these small fires burn out. This helps to stop very large fires happening, as some of the fuel has been used up.

G *The stream acts as a fire break to stop the fire spreading.*

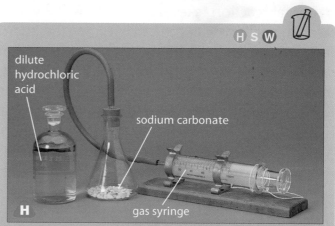

Ⓗ Ⓢ Ⓦ

dilute hydrochloric acid

sodium carbonate

H

gas syringe

A soda–acid extinguisher releases a stream of carbon dioxide gas which forms a layer over the fire. A model fire extinguisher can be made by adding dilute acid to sodium carbonate (soda).

o How do the amounts of soda and acid affect the volume of carbon dioxide produced?

5 **a** What is a fire break?
   b Which side of the fire triangle is removed by a fire break?

6 Explain how letting small fires burn in forests helps to stop large fires happening.

7 Design a presentation to explain how to put out different types of fire. Ⓗ Ⓢ Ⓦ

I CAN...

o name the three sides of the fire triangle.
o explain how fire extinguishers work and why different types are needed.
o select the correct extinguisher for a fire.

Ⓗ Ⓢ Ⓦ

What is produced when fuels burn?

A **fuel** is a substance which contains energy that can be changed into heat energy. Wood, coal, oil, petrol and natural gas are all fuels. A fuel will not burn unless it is heated first, and has oxygen to burn. If there is no oxygen, there will be no fire.

> 1 What is a fuel? Give four examples.
> 2 A fire stops burning. Think of as many reasons as possible why this could happen.

A This reaction produces a lot of heat.

Candles are made from wax. Wax is a substance that contains a lot of carbon joined to hydrogen. When a candle burns, a chemical reaction takes place. To start the wax burning, you need to split some of the carbon from the hydrogen. This needs heat energy, which will usually come from a match. When the candle is burning, the carbon joins with oxygen from the air to make a new substance - carbon dioxide. When the carbon joins to the oxygen, a lot of heat is given out. The wax also has a lot of hydrogen in it. The hydrogen joins with oxygen to make another oxide - hydrogen oxide. This is better known as water. This reaction also gives out heat. The heat keeps the reaction going.

B Wax is the fuel when a candle burns.

> 3 Is the burning of a candle:
> a a physical change or a chemical reaction
> b a reversible or an irreversible reaction?
> 4 When a candle burns, carbon joins with oxygen. What new substance is made?
> 5 Why do we need heat from a match to start the reaction off?
> 6 What is the difference between the wax melting and burning?

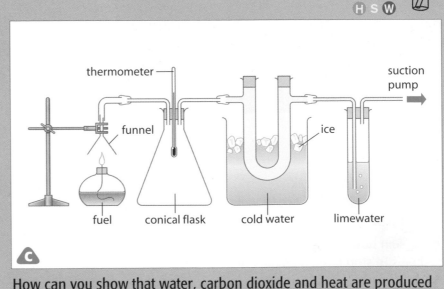

C

How can you show that water, carbon dioxide and heat are produced when different fuels are burnt?

Burning is also called **combustion**. We can summarise what happens when we burn a fuel by writing a word equation:

fuel + oxygen ⟶ carbon dioxide + water

Energy is not usually written in a word equation because it is *not* a chemical substance and so it is not a product.

Natural gas is another example of a fuel. Natural gas is mainly methane. Like candle wax, methane is a substance that contains carbon and hydrogen. Any chemical that is made of only carbon and hydrogen is called a **hydrocarbon**. When methane burns, it reacts with the oxygen in the air to make carbon dioxide and water. Heat and light energy are released.

methane + oxygen ⟶ carbon dioxide + water

In January 1986, shortly after take off, the space shuttle Challenger exploded. The large external tanks on the space shuttle contain hydrogen and oxygen. They react together to form water, and a lot of energy is released. A leak in the seal on one of the tanks caused the explosion.

7 Methane burns in air in a gas cooker:
  a What are the reactants?
  b What are the products?
  c Where does the energy come from to start the reaction off?

In photo E, the stall uses a diesel generator to provide electrical energy for the lights and the other electrical equipment. Diesel fuel is another hydrocarbon.

E *A diesel generator.*

8 What is a hydrocarbon?
9 a What fuel is used in the generator in photo E?
  b Write a word equation for the chemical reaction that takes place when this fuel burns.

I CAN...

o give some examples of fuels.
o explain that burning of fuels is a chemical reaction that produces carbon dioxide and water.

How can fuels cause pollution?

When methane burns completely, you get a clean blue flame. If there is not enough oxygen, the methane cannot burn completely and the flame turns yellow. Some of the carbon combines with a little oxygen to form carbon monoxide.

methane + oxygen ⟶ carbon monoxide + water

B A carbon monoxide detector.

Carbon monoxide is a very poisonous gas that is tasteless and doesn't smell. Gas fires and boilers should be serviced regularly to make sure that they are working properly and are not releasing carbon monoxide into the room. We can test for carbon monoxide by placing carbon monoxide detectors near to gas appliances.

If the oxygen supply is more restricted, the carbon in the fuel forms carbon powder, often called soot. When the fuel at Buncefield Oil Depot near Hemel Hempstead caught fire in December 2005, huge clouds of black sooty smoke were sent high into the air.

A The fuel in these torches is not burning efficiently.

C The Buncefield oil depot fire.

1 When is carbon monoxide produced from fuels rather than carbon dioxide?
2 Explain why it is important to have gas appliances serviced regularly. **H S W**
3 Some people have been killed by carbon monoxide without realising they were being poisoned. Explain why. **H S W**

H S W

o How long will the candle stay alight?
o Why does the candle go out?
o Which variables (factors) might affect the burning time?

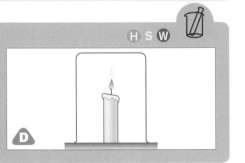

4 a What is soot? b When is soot produced?
5 List as many problems as you can think of that the explosion at Buncefield would have caused. **H S W**

I CAN...

o name the substances that may be formed when fuels burn.
o explain how carbon monoxide poisoning can be avoided. **H S W**
o describe some of the problems caused by burning fuels.

What are explosives and how do they work?

A chemical reaction becomes an explosion when:

- a large amount of gas is formed
- a lot of heat is released
- plenty of oxygen is available.

If the oxygen comes from the air, combustion takes place. If a substance already contains enough oxygen for the reaction to happen, decomposition occurs.

Chemicals which are designed to explode are called **explosives**. However, everyday chemicals such as flour or natural gas may explode if they are mixed with the right amount of oxygen and there is a source of energy, such as heat or an electrical spark.

> 1 What three factors make an explosion?
> 2 Does natural gas explode by combustion or decomposition? Explain your answer.

The first explosive ever used was gunpowder. It was invented in China about 1200 years ago. It needs to be lit for the explosive to work. Nitroglycerine is a very dangerous explosive. Knocking or dropping a bottle of nitroglycerine can provide enough energy to start the explosive reaction. Nitroglycerine is **unstable**.

In 1865, Alfred Nobel (1833–1896) opened a factory to make nitroglycerine. The factory blew up, killing his brother. Nobel set about inventing a more stable explosive. Eventually, he invented dynamite, by soaking a type of clay with nitroglycerine.

A Fireworks have a source of oxygen mixed with the fuel.

!

The power of explosives is due to the speed of the reaction, not the amount of energy released. Many breakfast cereals give out about 1600 kJ/100 g. The explosive, TNT, contains 1500 kJ/100 g!

> 3 Use ideas about the fire triangle to explain why:
>   a methane can explode if the conditions are right
>   b dynamite is safer than nitroglycerine.
> 4 Nitroglycerine is made of carbon, hydrogen, oxygen and nitrogen. Suggest the names of three gases that could be made when it explodes.

Are explosives a good or bad thing?

Explosives are chemicals that react very violently.

Exploding gas was a real problem for miners until the Davy lamp was invented. A fine wire mesh around the candle stopped the explosions.

A

Explosions often cause fires but they can also be used to put out fires! An oil well is a non-stop supply of fuel. Explosives can be used to blow out the flames. The blast of air cools the oil enough to let the oil workers stop the leak.

B

HowScienceWorks

C *Dynamite is used today to blast rock out of quarries, build roads through hills and knock down old buildings quickly.*

D *Gunpowder is still used in fireworks, and flash powder, containing magnesium, is used for special effects in films.*

E *Explosives can also be used to kill or injure in gun crime, terrorist attacks and war.*

HAVE YOUR SAY

Would the world be a better place if all explosives were banned? Discuss your ideas and give your opinions.

1 For each of the pictures on this page, explain whether the explosion is useful or harmful.
2 For each useful explosion, discuss whether you could achieve the same effect without using an explosive.

It is **estimated** that an average household in the UK produces 24 kilograms of rubbish each week. An estimate is a calculation using rough figures. So our homes produce about 30 million *tonnes* of waste each year. Industries produce about 400 million tonnes of waste. A lot of this waste ends up in **landfill sites**.

Some household rubbish is collected from our homes. Larger items and dangerous liquids need to be taken to a household waste recycling centre. There are different areas for different things.

A These photos show how a landfill site has grown between 2002 and 2007.

B A household waste recycling centre.

Putting items in different areas at the centre helps things to be recycled. Solids, like metal, glass and wood can all be recycled. Things that cannot be recycled are taken to a landfill site. Liquids do not go to landfill sites because many liquids harm the environment.

> **!** Dustcarts used to collect dust! Most people used to burn coal in their houses to keep warm. The dust and ashes were collected. Today, most people use oil, natural gas or electricity to heat their homes.

1 a How much rubbish is produced per household per week in the UK?

  b Estimate how much rubbish is produced per *person* per week in the UK? Show your working.

  c Do you think the amount of rubbish taken to landfill sites will go up or down in the future? Give a reason for your answer.

  d How would you check your prediction?

2 Old paint should not be thrown out in rubbish that is collected. Why not?

3 Think of a plus, a minus, and an interesting point about this statement: All rubbish should be picked up from our homes.

What are the differences between solids, liquids and gases?

In a household waste recycling centre, solids, liquids and gases are all stored separately. This is because they all have different **properties** and need to be handled in different ways. Solids, liquids are gases are the three **states of matter**.

Solids

Once useful materials have been removed at a recycling centre, the rest of the solid waste is taken to a landfill site.

Solids stay in one place, unless they are pushed or pulled. So the solids in the truck stay in place when they are transported. Solids do not **flow**.

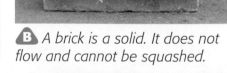

A An open truck is used to carry solid waste to a landfill site.

The **volume** of an object is the amount of space that it takes up. It is measured in **cubic centimetres** (**cm³**). Bits of a solid don't change their volumes. In other words, they cannot be squashed.

We say that any object that is heavy for its volume is **dense**. Solids are often dense.

> 1 Name the three states of matter.
> 2 What properties of solids make them useful for building houses?
> 3 Why can solid waste be left in piles at a landfill site?

B A brick is a solid. It does not flow and cannot be squashed.

Liquids

It would be very difficult to transport liquid waste in an open truck like the one in photo A. The liquid would slosh about as it was moved. This shows us one of the important properties of liquids – they flow.

Liquids need to be transported in sealed containers. They are often carried in tankers. The fact that liquids flow makes it easy for them to be pumped into and out of tankers.

C Waste liquids like sewage are easily pumped into a tanker and transported.

Liquids don't change their volumes – they cannot be squashed. Liquids are quite dense but usually less dense than solids.

4 Describe two properties of liquids.

5 If harmful substances get into the earth they can kill plants. Explain why liquids are not taken to landfill sites. Use a property of liquids in your answer. Ⓗ Ⓢ Ⓦ

D *Liquids flow but cannot be squashed.*

Gases

These gas cylinders have been left at a recycling centre. They may still contain flammable gases so they are stored away from other areas.

Gases are stored in tightly sealed containers because they flow very easily, and spread out to fill whatever container they are in. A slight break in the seal of the container will let all the gas escape.

Another reason for storing a gas in cylinders is that a gas does not have a fixed volume. You can squash lots of gas into a small cylinder. Some of the cylinders in photo E contained propane, which is burned in gas cookers. You can cook for many hours using a single cylinder.

Gases are not very dense. They are all less dense than liquids.

E *Gas cylinders.*

6 Put these substances in order of density, most dense first: iron, carbon dioxide, water.

7 Draw a table to show the differences between solids, liquids and gases. Use these headings: keeps its shape, keeps its volume, flows, how dense it is. Ⓗ Ⓢ Ⓦ

8 Look at drawing F. What do you think of Ravi's statement? (*Hint*: think about the differences between a single grain of sand and a lorry load of sand.) Ⓗ Ⓢ Ⓦ

SAND IS A LIQUID!

RAVI

F

I CAN...

○ classify substances as one of the three states of matter based on their properties (if they flow, if they keep their volumes and how dense they are). Ⓗ Ⓢ Ⓦ

What is a theory?

We can all understand that different items are placed in different areas of a household waste recycling centre because they have different properties. However, a scientist will want to understand *why* certain items have certain properties.

Scientists collect **data** (**observations** from experiments). For example some observations about ice are:
- it keeps its shape
- it cannot be squashed
- it turns into liquid water when it is warmed up.

A *This ice sofa will keep its shape and not be squashed when people sit on it. But the room needs to be kept cold!*

> **1** Write down two observations about liquids. (*Hint*: you may need to look back at pages 92 and 93.)

Scientists think about the observations and try to find an idea that explains them. They often have to use their imaginations. For instance, you might try to explain what happens when ice melts by imagining that you have a very powerful microscope that can see inside the ice.

> **2** Look at the cartoon.
> **a** What is the observation that this person is trying to explain?
> **b** What is his idea to explain the observation?

B *Observation: If you heat ice, it disappears and water runs away from it.*

Idea: Ice is made of lots of little boxes with water in them. The heat breaks open the boxes, so the water can run out.

Scientists can never really know if their ideas are right. A good idea is one that can explain why things happen. It can also be used to make **predictions** about what will happen. These predictions can then be tested using experiments.

If an idea has been tested and still works, it is called a **theory**. The data used to show whether a theory is right (or wrong) is called **evidence**. As more data is collected, a theory may need to be changed or scrapped altogether.

> **3** Look at the cartoon again.
> **a** Write down three more things that the idea about solids, liquids and gases would have to explain. (*Hint*: you may need to look back at pages 92 and 93.)
> **b** How well does the idea explain these things?
> **c** Why do you think scientists do not believe the idea?

One of the most important theories in science explains the differences between solids, liquids and gases. This theory explains a lot of observations.

Observation: It is very difficult ▶ to squash a solid or a liquid. It is quite easy to squash a gas.

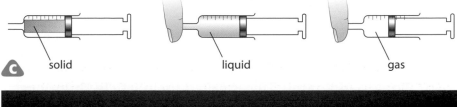

C solid   liquid   gas

Observation: You can make an ▶ orange drink using squash and water. The colour and flavour spread out. If you add more water, you dilute the drink. If you add enough water, you will not be able to see the orange colour any more.

D

Observation: If a sealed container of gas gets too hot, it explodes. ▼

Observation: If you put a purple crystal into water, it starts to dissolve and turn the water purple. If you leave the water long enough, the purple spreads out through the water without stirring. ▼

E

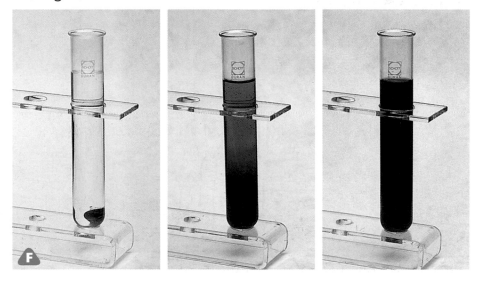

F

4 Give a reason why gas cylinders should be stored in shaded areas at a household recycling centre. Ⓗ Ⓢ Ⓦ

5 a What is an observation? Give an example.
  b What is a theory? Give an example.
  c What is a prediction? Give an example. Ⓗ Ⓢ Ⓦ

6 Write down three things that a theory about solids, liquids and gases should be able to explain. Ⓗ Ⓢ Ⓦ

I CAN...

o explain the meanings of the words observation, theory and prediction, and give examples. Ⓗ Ⓢ Ⓦ

o describe some of the things that a theory about solids, liquids and gases should be able to explain. Ⓗ Ⓢ Ⓦ

What is particle theory?

There is a theory that can explain the different properties of solids, liquids and gases. This is called the **particle theory** or particle model. It says that all things are made of tiny pieces called **particles** that are constantly moving. Solids, liquids and gases have different arrangements of particles, which give them their special properties.

Solids have particles that are very close together. The particles can vibrate (jiggle around) but are fixed in their places so they can't move past each other. That's why solids keep their shapes.

The particles in a **liquid** are close to one another but can move past each other. That's why liquids flow.

In **gases**, the particles are far apart and can move anywhere by themselves. That's why gases spread all over the place and fill any container they are in.

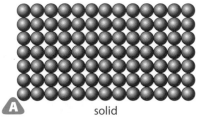

A   solid

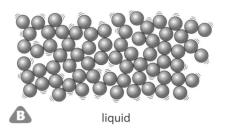

B   liquid

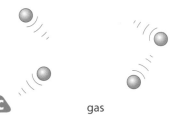

C   gas

2 What decides whether something is a solid, a liquid or a gas?

Explaining the properties

This machine is used to move rubbish around at the recycling centre.

Things can only be squashed if the particles get closer together. In a solid, the particles are already very close together. This makes it very difficult for the volume of a solid to be made smaller.

3 Explain why the grabber of the rubbish-mover is made of a solid.

This tube is filled with liquid, which pushes out the piston to move the grabber. The liquid can change shape and flow along pipes into the tube, but it can't be squashed and so it is able to push the piston out.

piston

The tyres are filled with a gas so that they are squashy and give a comfortable ride.

The grabber is solid. It needs to keep its shape and not get squashed.

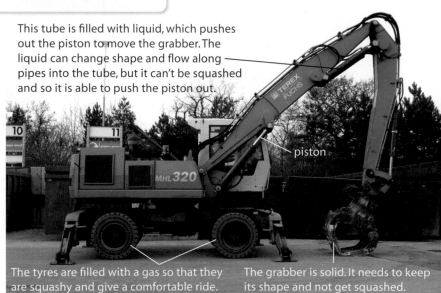

D *A recycling centre rubbish mover. This machine is used to move and squash rubbish at a recycling centre.*

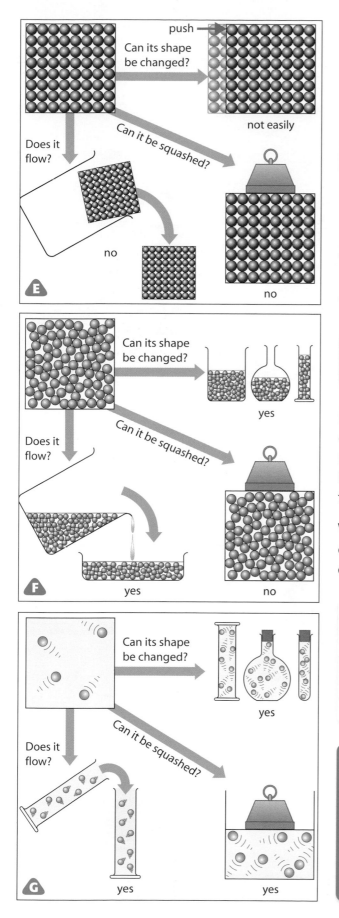

Solids have a fixed shape because the particles are held tightly together by forces, called **bonds**. These bonds are very strong and stop the particles from moving around. The particles are fixed in place and can only vibrate. This stops the solid flowing.

4 What holds the particles of a solid together?

Liquids cannot be squashed because the particles in a liquid are already close together. However, the particles can move past each other quite easily. The bonds in a liquid are weak enough to let the particles move past each other but strong enough to hold them close together.

5 Explain why a liquid can move the shovel of the rubbish-mover.

Particles in a gas are very far apart and move very quickly in all directions. The particles are able to move all over the place because there are no bonds between them. Therefore, a gas does not have a fixed volume or shape.

When we squash a gas, the particles are moved closer together. The more the gas is squashed, the closer together the particles will get.

6 Why would a gas not be suitable to fill the tube that moves the piston in the rubbish-mover?
7 Why can gas particles spread out to fill any space?
8 Describe how the particles move in solids, liquids and gases.

I CAN...

o recall how the particle theory says the particles in solids, liquids and gases are arranged. H S W
o describe how materials have different properties depending on how their particles are arranged. H S W

7Gd That stinks!

How do smells spread?

Seventy five percent of household waste in the UK ends up in landfill sites. These are ugly, take up room and smell!

When waste rots it naturally gives off gases (including smelly ones), which spread through the air. Even if the air is not moving, you still smell them. This is because the smelly particles move on their own, and spread through the air particles without anything moving them. This spreading of particles is called **diffusion**.

> **1 a** What is diffusion? **b** Give an example.

A A landfill site in Staveley, Derbyshire.

How could you measure the speed of diffusion through air?
- If your teacher opens a smelly bin, how long would the smell take to reach the back of the room? Make a prediction.
- How would you test your prediction? Would you need a smelly bin or could you use something else as a model for the bin?

Diffusion also happens in liquids. Pools of rainwater can collect in landfill sites. Chemicals in the waste dissolve in the water and spread through the water, without anything mixing them.

Diffusion is slower in liquids because the particles move more slowly than in a gas. There is also less space between liquid particles for other particles to move into.

> **2** Which is quicker, diffusion in liquids or gases? Explain why.
> **3** Look at photo C. What evidence is there that something has dissolved in the water?

C Some tea has dissolved and diffused through the water.

How could you find out how the speed of diffusion in liquids is affected by the temperature?
o How would you observe or measure the speed of diffusion?
o How many different temperatures would you try?

Solving landfill problems

The people who run landfill sites try to stop ponds of water forming. They make sure that rainwater, and any liquids formed in the waste, are drained away from the site.

Often the waste is covered in a layer of clay to stop the gases escaping into the air. A plastic sheet can be put under the clay to make sure that the gases don't get out. This sheet cannot be made of any old plastic since gases can diffuse through many plastics.

E A plastic sheet is used to help stop gases escaping from a landfill site.

4 Plastic sheets are also put underneath waste in some landfill sites. Suggest why. Ⓗ Ⓢ Ⓦ

5 Mingrui put some cola in an old plastic squash bottle. The cola is now flat. Why? Think of as many reasons as you can. Ⓗ Ⓢ Ⓦ

You need to get rid of the gases from waste somehow. Wells are drilled through the clay layer and into the rotting waste. The gases can then be piped out. This is possible because of their properties. Most of the gas is methane, a gas that helps to cause global warming. The methane is burnt (sometimes in a mini power plant to produce electricity). Burning also destroys any smelly gases.

F Methane from a landfill site is burnt.

6 Why is methane from waste burnt?
7 Which of these are examples of diffusion?
  a You can smell the aroma of coffee when you open a new jar of granules.
  b You stir your tea to get the sugar to dissolve.
  c A breeze is blowing and you smell the cooking from a barbecue next door.
  d A baby has a dirty nappy. You can smell it from across the room.

I CAN...

o describe what diffusion is.
o use the particle theory to explain why diffusion is faster in gases than liquids. Ⓗ Ⓢ Ⓦ

What causes pressure in gases?

The methane gas produced in landfill sites can be dangerous. Gases flow very easily and so the methane can flow all through a landfill site and collect in pockets. Sparks can cause the gas to explode or the build-up of gas in a pocket can cause the ground above it to burst or crack. So, it is important to get the methane out of landfill sites.

> **1** Give two reasons why it is important to get rid of the gases inside a landfill site. Ⓗ Ⓢ Ⓦ

A These cracks were caused by gas collecting inside the landfill.

When a gas builds up in a closed-in space it creates a 'pushing' known as **pressure**. Pressure is caused by particles. The moving particles bump into each other and hit the sides of their container. The forces of the particles hitting the sides cause pressure. If more particles hit the sides, there is more pressure.

Think about a balloon. As it is blown up, more and more gas particles are put inside. The pressure gets bigger because there are more particles hitting the sides of the balloon. Eventually the pressure becomes so great that the balloon bursts.

> **2** What causes pressure in a container of gas? Ⓗ Ⓢ Ⓦ
>
> **3** Explain how the cracks in photo A were formed. Ⓗ Ⓢ Ⓦ

Air pressure

The air particles around us put pressure on us. This is called **air pressure**. We can't feel this pressure because we are so used to it. However, we can see its effects.

When you blow up a balloon, more particles are blown into it. This increases the pressure.

This makes the rubber stretch and the balloon gets bigger. When the pressure inside it is the same as the air pressure outside it, the balloon stops expanding.

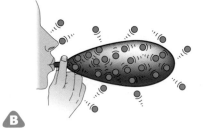

B

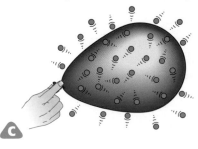

C

> **4** Why does the air put pressure on us? Ⓗ Ⓢ Ⓦ

Photo D shows a geyser that is only active in the mornings. At night, the air is very cold. In cold air the particles are close together and create more pressure. This pressure stops gases escaping from the geyser. In the morning, the air warms up and the air pressure is reduced. The gases suddenly escape, pushing boiling water up out of the ground too. The geyser lasts for about half an hour before all the boiling water has been used up.

escaping gases force boiling water to shoot out of the ground

If it were not for air pressure you could not suck things through a straw.

E

When you suck, you make the pressure inside your mouth lower than the pressure outside.

Air pressure from the atmosphere is pushing on the liquid in the glass.

This pressure is greater than the pressure inside your mouth, and it pushes the drink up the straw.

5 Explain how air pressure helps you to drink through a straw. **H S W**

D *The geysers at El Tatio, Chile, are the highest in the world.*

If you suck all the air out of something, you get a **vacuum**. A vacuum is a space where there are no particles at all, not even air particles.

Photo F shows two Magdeburg hemispheres. If the air is sucked out of these Magdeburg hemispheres, they are very difficult to pull apart. The pressure of the air on the outside of the hemispheres pushes them together.

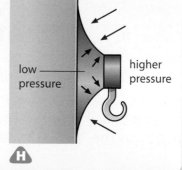

F

H S W 🍶

What do you think will happen if all the air is sucked out of this can?
o Explain your prediction using ideas about particles.

G

6 Why will the hook in drawing H stay fixed to the wall? **H S W**

7 Explain why **H S W** Magdeburg hemispheres stay together when there is a vacuum inside.

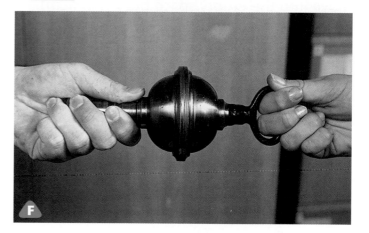

low pressure
higher pressure

H

I CAN...

o explain how gases cause pressure. **H S W**
o recall some effects of gas pressure.

What is the evidence for particle theory?

How**S**cience**W**orks

Scientists have to do a lot of creative thinking to come up with theories. The ancient Greek thinker Democritus did a 'thought experiment'. He imagined cutting a stone into two, then cutting the two halves into two, and keeping on doing this. He reasoned that you would end up with something that could not be divided any more – a particle. He thought that if you could keep dividing things you would eventually end up with nothing, which was impossible. He went on to say that he thought that particles were separated by empty space – a vacuum.

A *Democritus (c. 460 BCE – c. 370 BCE).*

B *Aristotle (384 BCE – 322 BCE).*

This theory explained how you could feel matter (it was made of something) and why matter could move (the particles could move into the empty space between them).

Another Greek, Aristotle, did not think you could have a vacuum. He thought that for something to be real it must be made of something. With these ideas in mind, Isaac Newton (1643–1727) imagined particles of a gas held in something called 'aether'.

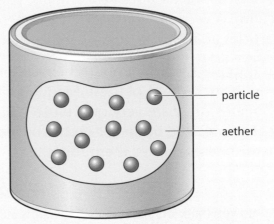

particle

aether

> **1** What observations did Democritus' theory explain?
> **2** Why did Aristotle not think you could have a vacuum?

C *Newton's idea about gas particles.*

Robert Boyle (1627–1691) reasoned that when you squashed a gas, the aether must escape. He did an experiment. He took a certain mass of air in a sealed container and squashed it. He found that it still had the same mass. So the 'aether' had not escaped.

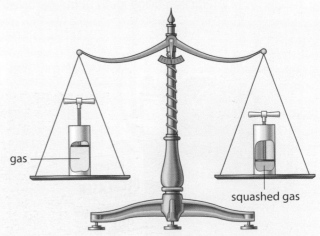

gas

squashed gas

> **!**
>
> Samuel Pepys wrote in his diary that King Charles II 'mightily laughed' when he heard that Boyle and others were 'spending time only in weighing of air'.

D *The gas and the squashed gas have the same mass.*

Next Boyle wondered whether the particles might be squashy, like springs. But there was a problem. What was between the coils of the unsquashed springs? It would be 'aether'. With 'aether' in the way, the gas could not be squashed *and* keep its mass.

So he decided that Democritus was right, and when you squashed a gas, the particles moved closer together into the empty space.

> **3** Draw a picture of Boyle's final theory about particles in gases.

Many scientists did not believe this. They agreed with Aristotle that a vacuum could not exist. In 1643 Italian Evangelista Torricelli (1608–1647) created a vacuum at the top of a sealed column of liquid and in 1654 German Otto von Guericke (1602–1686) showed that two teams of horses could not separate Magdeburg hemispheres (see page 101).

Many scientists continued to work on the problem, changing the theory as new evidence was discovered. This included showing that the particles moved but that they did not all move at the same speed.

These scientists included Albert Einstein (1879–1955). When tiny pollen grains float in water they are seen to jiggle about. Einstein said that this was because water particles were bumping into the pollen grains. Einstein's theory predicted how far a pollen grain would be moved by water particles. This was tested by J. B. Perrin (1870–1942) and found to be correct.

Today we can detect atoms using highly sensitive microscopes.

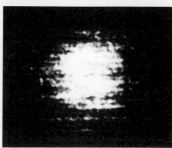

H A gold atom (×30 000 000).

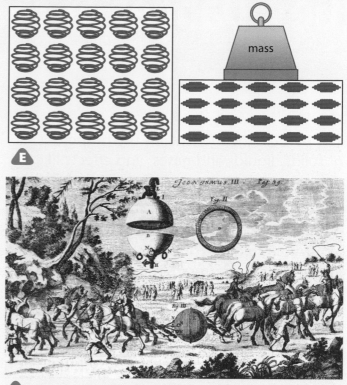

E

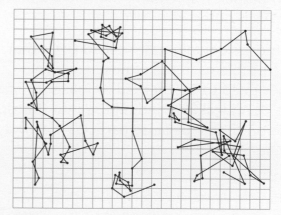

F *Von Guericke's experiment.*

> **4** How did von Guericke's experiment provide evidence for Boyle's theory?

G *Perrin's drawing of how some tiny grains moved. Each grain's position was noted using a dot every 30 seconds.*

> **5 a** What does drawing G show?
> **b** Why doesn't it show exactly the paths that the grains moved in?
> **6** What makes a good theory?
> **7** Find out what contribution Daniel Bernoulli (1700–1782) made to the particle theory.

HowScienceWorks

The particle theory explains the properties of solids, liquids and gases, and effects like diffusion and air pressure. People working at a household waste recycling centre must know about these properties so that waste is safely stored, sorted and disposed of.

Gas cylinders are stored out of direct sunlight. Making the gas too hot can make the cylinder explode. This is because the hotter the particles get, the faster they move and the harder they hit the sides of the container. This increases the pressure.

A spill of a dangerous liquid needs to be treated. This is often done by adding lots of water to dilute the liquid. Dilution occurs because the water particles mix with the other liquid particles, spreading them further away from each other.

Old fridges contain gases called CFCs that cause problems in the atmosphere. The fridges need to be checked to make sure the CFCs don't leak out and diffuse into the air. Diffusion occurs because particles are always moving about.

A The carbon dioxide cylinder in a drinks machine got too hot in the sun at a cricket match in Pakistan and exploded.

If chemicals get into someone's eyes, they can be diluted quickly with emergency eye wash. **B**

HAVE YOUR SAY

Only householders can use the recycling centre. Companies that want to dump waste need to take it to a landfill site and pay landfill tax. Some companies avoid this tax by just dumping their waste. This is called fly tipping. You can be fined up to £20 000 for fly tipping. Do you think this is reasonable?

1 How can the particle theory explain dilution?
2 Why do old fridges need to be carefully handled at a household waste recycling centre?
3 Another thing that the particle theory needs to explain is why solids get bigger when they are heated.
   a Suggest a way in which the particle theory could explain this.
   b How would you find out if you are right?

HowScienceWorks

Many of the materials around you come from the Earth. Some uses of Earth materials are obvious, such as stones used to make walls, or gravel used in footpaths. Some are not so obvious; for example, glass and toothpaste are made using limestone.

Early humans could only use the materials directly available around them. These materials had such a great effect on the way people lived that some historical periods are named after them.

Some rocks contain metal compounds, from which we obtain metals.

The engine is burning coal, which was mined from the ground.

Stones used for ballast spread the weight of the tracks and allow water to drain away.

B *Stone Age axe head.*

C *By about 2000 BCE humans had learned to extract metals like copper and tin from rocks to make bronze. Bronze tools and weapons were harder and more effective than stone ones. This is a bronze age axe head.*

D *Geologists study rocks to locate useful materials and to find out about the history of the Earth.*

1 a Write down as many different uses for rocks as you can.
  b For each of your uses listed in part **a**, suggest what properties the rock should have.
2 Rocks can be worn away. Suggest different ways in which rocks can wear away.
3 a Suggest why some people in the Stone Age might have investigated the properties of different rocks.
  b The rocks from which metals are extracted have to be dug out of the ground. Suggest why some people in the Bronze Age might have studied different types of rocks.

How can we describe rocks?

There are many different types of rock, and they have different uses. The uses of different rocks depend on their **properties**. Rocks are made of different **grains** that fit together. Each grain is made of one chemical. The chemicals in rocks are called **minerals**. Rocks are **mixtures** of different minerals.

The grains in rocks can be different sizes and shapes. The combination of sizes and shapes of grains is called the **texture** of the rock. Geologists classify rocks by the minerals they contain and by looking at the texture.

In some rocks the grains all fit together with no gaps. We say that the grains are **interlocking**. Interlocking grains are sometimes called **crystals**. Rocks made of interlocking grains are usually hard and do not wear away easily.

> **1 a** What is a mineral?
> **b** What is a grain?

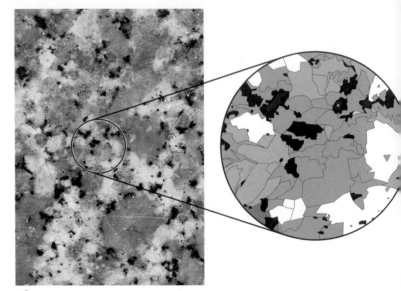

A Granite is made from three or four main minerals. It has interlocking grains. Granite is an example of an **igneous rock**. Igneous rocks form when molten (liquid) rock cools down.

B Gneiss (pronounced 'nice') is an example of a **metamorphic rock**. Metamorphic rocks have interlocking grains that are often lined up or arranged in bands. They form when existing rocks are heated or squashed.

In other rocks the grains are more rounded, and there are gaps between them. Rocks like this are not usually as strong as rocks made from interlocking crystals, and wear away more easily.

> **2** Write down the name of a rock that has:
> **a** rounded grains   **b** interlocking grains.

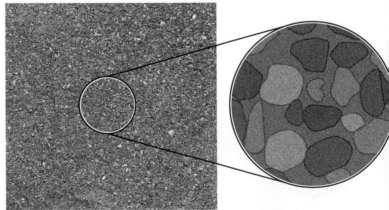

C Sandstone has rounded grains. The grains are mostly made of a mineral called quartz. Sandstone is an example of a **sedimentary rock**. Most sedimentary rocks are formed when tiny grains of existing rock become stuck together.

Rocks made of rounded grains can absorb water because it can get into the gaps between the grains. These rocks are said to be **porous**. Most porous rocks are also **permeable** (water can run through them).

3 Write down three ways in which granite is different from sandstone.

4 Why do rocks made from rounded grains absorb water?

5 Look at photo D. Suggest why pumice is porous but not permeable. **H S W**

D *Pumice has lots of air bubbles inside it. It is unusual because it is porous, but not permeable.*

In some parts of the country, the properties of different rocks affect what we see around us. Photo E shows low hills with higher hills behind. They look different because they are made of different rocks.

6 Look at photo E. Which type of rock wears away most easily? Explain your answer. **H S W**

E *The gentle hills in the foreground are made of sedimentary rocks. The higher hills beyond them are made from hard, igneous rocks.*

H S W !

Rocks are transparent if you slice them thinly enough! Geologists use microscopes to look at thin sections of rocks to learn about the minerals in them.

F *A thin section of granite seen through a microscope.*

H S W

How could you investigate whether some rocks are more permeable than others?
- How would you carry out a fair test?

I CAN...

- explain the difference between a rock and a mineral.
- describe the texture of different rocks.
- find out if a rock is porous. **H S W**

What happens to weathered pieces of rock?

Physical weathering breaks up rocks into smaller pieces, which usually get moved away from the place where they were formed. This movement of bits of rock is called **erosion**.

A Geologists are consulted when new road cuttings are made. They decide what needs to be done to make sure that weathered bits of rock will not fall onto the road.

C These rocks were carried down the river bed by a 'flash flood', when there was a lot of very fast-moving water.

If rocks fall into a stream or river, they can get **transported** (carried away). As they are moved by the water, the rock fragments knock against each other and wear away. This is called **abrasion**. The bits of rock or sand in streams or rivers are called **sediment**.

B As they were moved by the waves, the pebbles on this beach have been worn away and rounded by abrasion.

The size of sediment particles that can be carried by a river depends on how fast the water is moving. Faster-moving water can carry bigger pieces of rock. Sediments can also be carried by the wind. The wind can only move very small particles.

1 What is sediment?
2 How do rock fragments get worn away in streams and rivers?
3 a What happens to the shape of rocks that are transported in streams?
  b What do you think happens to their masses? Explain your answer.
4 Look at the rocks in photo C. Suggest why they are not rounded.

Glaciers are rivers of ice. They move very slowly, but they can transport very large pieces of rock. Rocks carried by glaciers also scrape away bits of rock from the land they are moving over. Rocks below the glacier are **abraded** into very small particles.

Sediments carried by water or ice are **deposited** (dropped) when the water slows down, or when the ice melts. Sediments carried by wind are deposited when the wind slows down.

These sharp ridges were formed when glaciers covered more of the land.

rocks deposited beside the glacier

bits of rock being carried on the surface of the glacier

D *The Mer de Glace, France.*

E *The water in this jar has just been swirled.*

F *The water in the jar has stopped moving.*

H S W

bluestones

There are two theories as to how the 5 tonne bluestones travelled 240 miles from Wales to Stonehenge; by people moving them or by glaciers.

H S W

How would you find out how far water can carry grains of rock? What would happen if you changed these things:

○ the flow of water
○ the width of the stream
○ the size of the grains of rock?

5 Why does the sand get deposited at the bottom of the jar in photo F?

6 After a rain storm, rivers often have a lot of fast-flowing water in them.
   a Why do flooded rivers usually look dirty?
   b Where has the dirt come from?
   c What happens when the water level drops?

7 You can show what happens when rocks are carried by water by shaking some sugar cubes in a jar.
   a Explain what will happen when the jar is shaken.
   b Explain how this can demonstrate what happens to rocks carried by water. H S W
   c In what ways is this not a good model for rocks in a stream? H S W

I CAN...

○ use a model to explain how bits of rock are transported and deposited. H S W

How are sedimentary rocks formed?

Sedimentary rocks are formed from sediments deposited on the beds of rivers or seas. Over a long period of time, more layers of sediment are deposited on top of the first one. As this happens, the newer layers on top squash the bottom layers. The pressure from these newer layers forces the grains of sediment closer together. This squashing (called **compaction**) squeezes the water out from the gaps between the grains. This can be shown by squeezing wet sand.

A The sandstone in these canyon walls was made from grains of sand. Much later, the sandstone was weathered and eroded by flash floods.

B When wet grains of sand are squashed together, water runs out and the grains of sand stick together.

If the water in the sediment contains dissolved minerals, the minerals can crystallise in the gaps as a 'glue' that **cements** the grains together. Compaction and **cementation** together change sediments into sedimentary rocks.

Fossils form when dead plants or animals become covered in a layer of sediment before they rot away. If the sediments that are covering the remains change into sedimentary rocks, the remains of the animals and plants can also turn into rock, but they keep their shapes.

C The fossilised remains of trilobites in limestone.

1 What do these words mean?
   a compaction   b cementation
2 Where does the glue come from that holds the grains together in a sedimentary rock?
3 What is a fossil?

Sometimes a layer of sediment will be made of broken up bits of shell. This can often happen in the sea, when creatures with shells die on the sea bed. The shells get broken by the moving water and other layers of sediment squashing them from above. If the layer of shells is squashed by many other layers of sediment and is cemented, it can turn into **limestone**.

Limestone is mainly made of a white mineral formed from **calcium carbonate**. However, other minerals may also be present in the rock (formed, for example, from sand or mud mixed with the shells) and so limestones can be different colours.

4 a What is the main chemical in limestone called?

b What colour is this chemical?

c Why are some limestones yellow or grey?

D *You can see the shapes of some of the shells that formed this limestone.*

Calcium carbonate is slightly soluble in water. Some limestones are formed when dissolved calcium carbonate is left behind after some of the water has evaporated. **Oolite** is an example of a limestone which was formed in this way.

Ⓗ Ⓢ Ⓦ
Carbonates react with acid, and give off carbon dioxide gas and water. Other minerals in rocks do not react with acid.

○ How would you find out how much calcium carbonate is found in two different sorts of limestone?

○ How could you make sure your test is fair?

5 Some fossils are made of a mineral called pyrite. Pyrite does not react with acid. Ⓗ Ⓢ Ⓦ

a How could a geologist use acid to get a pyrite fossil out of limestone?

b Why wouldn't this work if the fossil was in sandstone?

6 Draw a flowchart to show how sedimentary rock is made from a layer of sediment. Ⓗ Ⓢ Ⓦ

Ⓗ Ⓢ Ⓦ
Limestone is an important raw material for making cement and concrete. The ancient Egyptians used concrete as long ago as 2500 BCE.

E *Chalk is a kind of limestone formed from the remains of microscopic organisms that collected at the bottom of shallow lagoons. Chalk is white because it does not contain any impurities.*

F *Oolite.*

I CAN...

○ explain how sedimentary rocks are formed.

○ explain what fossils are and how they are formed.

What evidence can we find in sedimentary rocks?

HowScienceWorks

Sedimentary rocks are all formed from sediments, but they can form from different kinds of sediments and in different places. Geologists examine sedimentary rocks to find evidence that helps them to work out how they formed.

Rocks formed from sediments often have layers. Layers in rocks form because rivers do not always transport the same kinds of sediments. When the river is flowing slowly, it may only be able to carry mud or tiny pieces of sand. The layers of sediment deposited by the river will form rock with very small grains. When the river flows fast it can carry larger pieces of rock. The sediments deposited when it slows down will be larger, and will form rock with larger grains.

A *The river has cut down through these rocks, allowing us to see the layers.*

1 Look at photo A. How can you tell that the rocks were formed from sediments?

2 Why do sedimentary rocks often form layers?

B *The rock fragments that formed this conglomerate were carried by fast-flowing water.*

C *This mudstone was formed from very fine grains.*

D *This breccia (pronounced '**bretch**-ee-ah') has sharp-edged fragments.*

3 List the differences between the conglomerate and the mudstone in photos B and C.

4 a What evidence is there in photo B for the speed of the water that carried the fragments?

   b What can you say about the speed of the water that carried the fragments that made the mudstone?

5 a List the similarities and differences between the conglomerate in photo B and the breccia in photo D.

   b What are the differences in the way they were formed?

Coal, **oil** and **natural gas** are important stores of energy. They are called **fossil fuels** because they were formed from the remains of plants and animals. Coal was formed when swamps, like the one in drawing E, were buried by sediments. The plants did not rot, but eventually became transformed into coal. Oil and natural gas were formed when tiny sea plants and animals became buried by sediments.

E This is how a swamp may have looked 300 million years ago.

F Sometimes fossils of parts of plants are found in coal.

6 What evidence could the artist have used to draw the plants in drawing E?

7 Look at photo G.
  a Where were these rocks formed? (Choose from 'beneath a lake', 'in a desert', 'under the sea'.)
  b Explain your answer to part **a**.
  c What size grains would you expect the rock to have? Explain your answer.

8 Look at photo A. Will the oldest rocks be at the top or the bottom? Explain your answer.

The red colour is due to a chemical called iron oxide, which forms in dry conditions.

The diagonal lines show that the sediments were deposited by moving air.

G Some rocks can tell geologists lots of things about the way the rock was formed.

I CAN...

o use evidence from rocks to explain how they were formed.

How can we tell what rocks are in the ground? HowScienceWorks

A *This rig extracts oil from rocks beneath the North Sea. But how did the oil company know where to drill?*

We use many rocks and minerals from the Earth. Mining and oil companies need to know where to look for the materials they want. Geological maps show where different rocks can be found on the surface of the land, but geologists also need to know what rocks are beneath the surface.

> **1** Why is it important to know what kinds of rock there are under the ground?

The first geological map of the UK was drawn by Christopher Packe (1686–1749) in 1743. It showed the rocks in Kent. Maps of other areas were drawn during the rest of the century, but they all just showed the rocks at the surface.

Other scientists drew maps of the layers of sedimentary rocks based on information from mines. John Strachey (1671–1743) drew cross-sections of parts of the Somerset coal field. He found that the fossils changed as you got deeper into the mine. He also noticed that a coal layer (or seam) in one mine could have the same fossils as a seam at a different depth in another mine. He decided that seams with the same fossils had been formed at the same time, and that earth movements had caused the seams to be at different depths.

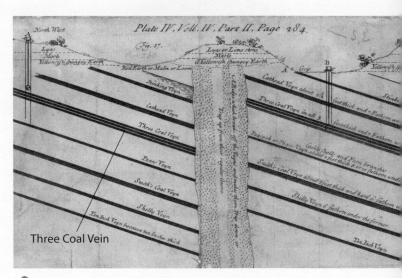

Three Coal Vein

B *A cross-section by John Strachey.*

> **2** Look at drawing B. How do you think Strachey worked out what happened to the Three Coal Vein between the two mines shown on his drawing?

> **3** The positions of most of the coal seams are estimates.
> **a** Explain why the positions of the top three coal seams are likely to be the most accurate.
> **b** Suggest how Strachey estimated the positions of the seams below the Three Coal Vein.

William Smith (1769–1839) was a surveyor. His job was to survey land to help landowners to improve their land or to find out if it was worth mining for coal. He saw, as Strachey had, that the pattern of coal seams was repeated in many different mines, and he wondered if the same was true of all rocks, not just the coal seams.

In 1794, construction of a canal was started to transport the coal from the Somerset mines. William Smith got the job of Official Surveyor. While he was surveying the countryside for the canal company, he made many detailed observations of the rocks he saw. He also travelled around the rest of the country, on foot or by horse-drawn carriage, to examine the rocks. He decided to publish a geological map of the whole of England and Wales by adding colour to a normal map. His map was published in 1815. It showed the relative ages of the rocks.

Unfortunately, other people copied his map and sold it, and he went bankrupt. The importance of his work was not recognised by other geologists for many years, but in 1831 he was awarded a medal by the Geological Society of London.

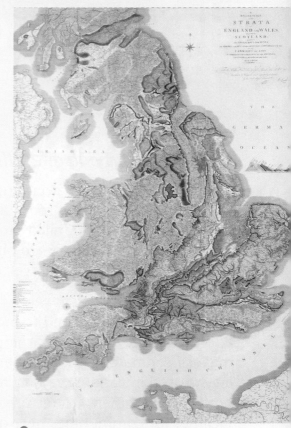

C William Smith's map.

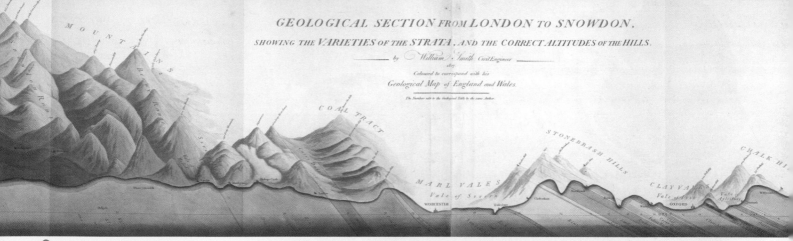

D Smith also drew some geological sections that showed what happened to the rocks under the ground.

4 Look at drawing D. What has happened to the rocks shown since they were first formed? Explain your answer.

5 a Suggest as many differences as you can between the way William Smith worked and the way a modern geologist might work.

 b Suggest some parts of the Earth we can explore today that could not be explored in Smith's time.

E Geologists in Antarctica. They are using equipment that will automatically send data across the world.

HowScienceWorks

How does quarrying affect the environment?

Sand, gravel and other stones used in making concrete, in buildings and in making roads are known as **aggregates**. Between 250 and 300 million tonnes of aggregates are used in the UK each year. They are obtained by dredging sand from the sea bed, digging up gravel, or quarrying solid rock and breaking it up.

The government has tried to increase the amount of aggregates recycled by charging a levy on new material. This makes new material more expensive. The money from this levy is used in various ways to reduce the effects of quarrying on the environment, to restore old quarries, and to provide facilities for communities near quarries.

> It's dreadful living near a quarry – there is noise and dust everywhere!

B

> The company are great – they told us as soon as they found these prehistoric remains, and they have given us enough time to study them properly.

C

> We should just make buildings out of metal instead, then we wouldn't need these quarries.

D

HAVE YOUR SAY

Should we be quarrying for the aggregates we need in this country, or should we import them from other countries?

1 a How are sand and gravel formed?
  b What are aggregates used for?
  c Why aren't quarries dug everywhere in the UK?

2 How does quarrying affect the environment? List as many ways as you can.

3 a Suggest some advantages of recycling aggregates.
  b Why might recycled aggregates cost more to produce than freshly quarried material?

4 What are the advantages of quarrying the aggregates we need in this country instead of importing them?

7la Green living

HowScienceWorks

Some people think about science in their everyday lives. Rebecca and her family use their knowledge of energy to help them live in a certain way. Almost everything that happens needs a store of energy. **Fuels** such as **coal**, **oil** and **natural gas** are **energy resources**. Fuel is needed to cook food and keep our homes warm, and to keep cars, buses and trains moving. The cells in our bodies use food as a fuel to keep us alive.

A

> **1** Write down all the things in the kitchen that energy is being used for.

Most of the energy resources we use in our homes, cars or schools will run out one day. Many scientists think that using these energy resources is also contributing to **global warming**. This theory says that the Earth is getting warmer, and this could lead to huge problems in many countries, such as flooding and starvation.

Rebecca and her family try to live **sustainably**. This means that they try to live without harming the things around them. Their house and the way they live do not contribute to global warming. The rest of us can also change the way we live to reduce our effects on our surroundings.

> **2 a** Write down five things you did today that needed energy resources.
> **b** Write down one thing you could do to reduce the amount of energy resources you use.
> **3** Should you be doing anything to help to reduce global warming? Write down some things you would need to find out about before you could answer this question properly.

B *Rebecca and her family live in the Hockerton Housing Project – a development of sustainable houses built in Nottinghamshire.*

How can we use less fossil fuel?

Most scientists who study the climate think that fossil fuels are helping to make the Earth warmer because a gas called carbon dioxide is made when they burn. Extra carbon dioxide in the atmosphere makes the Earth warmer.

We can reduce the amount of carbon dioxide we add to the atmosphere by using fewer fossil fuels. This will also help to make our supply of fossil fuels last longer.

A You could reduce your household energy use by 3% by putting on a jumper and keeping your house 1°C cooler!

B Cooking vegetables in a microwave oven uses less than half the energy it takes to boil them in a pan.

C Ordinary homes can have insulation added so that less heat escapes.

D The houses at Hockerton are designed to be warmed by the Sun. The people who live there do not need to use any energy from fossil fuels or electricity to heat the houses.

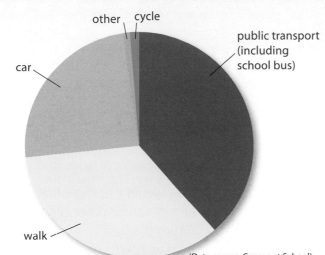

(Data source: Census at School)

E *How secondary school children get to school.*

30% of car journeys are not really necessary. People would be healthier if they walked or cycled instead of using the car, and pollution would be less.

A rail passenger travelling by high speed train uses about half the energy of someone travelling the same distance by car.

G

H *This car uses 7.2 litres of petrol to travel 100 km. The same car with a diesel engine would use only 6.0 litres of diesel.*

I *This car uses 5.9 litres of petrol to travel 100 km. The same car with a diesel engine would use only 4.5 litres of diesel.*

F *A bus uses more fuel than a car, but it can carry a lot more people. And think how many people a train can carry!*

1 Why should we try to use less fossil fuels?

2 a Make a list of all the ways of using less ⒽⓈⓌ energy shown on these pages.

   b Add some more suggestions of your own.

3 Look at the list you made in question 2. ⒽⓈⓌ

   a Put a ring around all the changes you could make.

   b Underline the changes that your parents could make.

   c How could the government persuade people to make changes?

4 Danny says 'We should persuade more people to use bicycles to get to school instead of coming on the bus'. ⒽⓈⓌ

   a Look at chart E. Suggest why Danny thinks it is most useful to persuade the people using public transport.

   b Explain how Danny's idea would help to use less fossil fuels.

   c Explain why persuading the car users would be more useful.

5 Think of a plus, a minus, and an interesting point about these statements: ⒽⓈⓌ

   a No-one should own a car.

   b All new houses should be designed like the ones at Hockerton.

I CAN...

○ explain why it is important to reduce the amount of fossil fuels we use. ⒽⓈⓦ

○ describe some ways of doing this.

●●●123

What other energy resources are available?

A **biomass fuel** is one that is obtained from plants or from animal waste. This includes straw, cow dung, sewage and even rubbish. As these things rot away, methane gas is produced. This is the same gas as natural gas.

Wood is a biomass fuel. It has been used for thousands of years for heating and cooking. It is a **renewable** resource because new trees can be grown to replace the ones that have been used. Other crops can also be grown to be used as fuels.

Plants use carbon dioxide from the atmosphere when they grow. This carbon dioxide is released when the plants are burnt, so overall the amount of carbon dioxide in the atmosphere does not change much when biomass fuels are used.

Energy resources that do not produce carbon dioxide

Nuclear power stations use energy stored in metals such as **uranium**. Uranium gives off large amounts of **radiation**, which can cause cancer. The radiation can be used in power stations to generate electricity. Uranium will run out eventually. It is non-renewable.

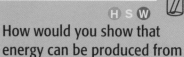

How would you show that energy can be produced from rotting biomass?

o How could you use this idea to keep plants warm in a greenhouse?

A

1 What are biomass fuels?

2 Why can biomass fuels be described as renewable resources?

3 Why is uranium a non-renewable fuel?

B *Wind turbines can be built out at sea or on land.*

The wind, moving water and the Sun can be used as energy resources. They are renewable resources.

Wind turbines are used to generate electricity from the wind. The wind turns the large blades, and the blades turn a generator.

Wind turbines would need to cover an area the size of the Isle of Wight to produce the same amount of energy as one nuclear power station.

Flowing water can be used to generate electrical energy in a **hydroelectric power** station. Waves and tides can also be used to generate electricity.

Solar power uses sunlight. **Solar panels** absorb energy from the Sun and transfer this energy to heat water. Some houses have solar panels to make hot water for the house.

4 a What are the advantages of using wind power? H S W

b What are the disadvantages? H S W

5 Write down three examples of using water to generate electricity.

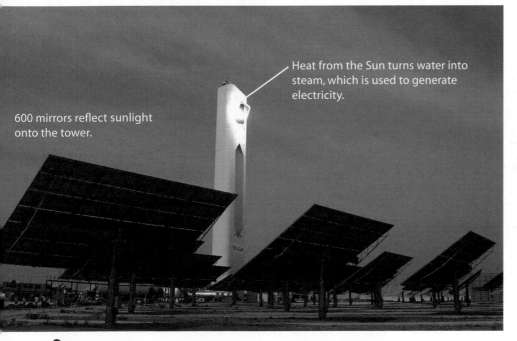

600 mirrors reflect sunlight onto the tower.

Heat from the Sun turns water into steam, which is used to generate electricity.

C *This solar power station is near Seville, in Spain.*

D *The solar cells on the roof of the houses at Hockerton provide electricity for the people who live there.*

Solar cells are used to transfer energy from the Sun directly into electricity. These can be used to provide electricity for small towns but they take up a lot of space. Solar cells are mainly used in small electrical items like calculators.

In some places, rocks under the ground are hot. Water can be heated by pumping it through the rocks. This is called **geothermal power**.

6 What is the difference between solar panels and solar cells?

7 Choose one of the renewable energy sources mentioned on these pages. Describe how it works and what you think its advantages and disadvantages are. H S W

I CAN...

○ explain why people are interested in using renewable energy resources. H S W

○ give some examples of non-renewable and renewable energy resources.

Green transport

How can we replace fossil fuels for transport?

Burning fossil fuels adds carbon dioxide to the atmosphere. Using other energy resources for transport can help to reduce the amount of carbon dioxide in the atmosphere.

Most cars that normally run on diesel (rather than petrol) can use **biodiesel** instead. This fuel is made from vegetable oil. However there are not many filling stations selling biodiesel in the UK, and some of those only sell normal diesel with a little biodiesel mixed in. A **biofuel** is any fuel made from plants or from animal wastes.

Vehicles can also run on electricity. Battery-powered cars need to be recharged from the mains electricity supply. At the moment these cars cannot go very far before they need to be recharged.

Electric vehicles can also be powered by **fuel cells**. Many fuel cells use fuels such as hydrogen gas, which combines with oxygen and produces electricity. The only waste gas is water vapour. Oxygen and hydrogen can be obtained from water, using electricity.

Using electric vehicles only helps to reduce global warming if the electricity used to charge the batteries or to provide fuel for the fuel cells is made using renewable resources.

B *This battery-powered car is used by all the families who live in the Hockerton houses.*

1 What is a biofuel?
2 a How can using biofuels help to reduce the amount of carbon dioxide in the atmosphere?
   b How can using electric vehicles help?
3 Very few cars use biodiesel or electricity.
   a Suggest as many reasons for this as you can.
   b What could be done to encourage more drivers to use 'green' vehicles? Who would have to carry out your suggestions? **H S W**

I CAN...

○ explain that biofuels are made from plants or animal wastes.
○ describe two ways in which electricity can be used to power vehicles.
○ identify some fuel choices that people can make. **H S W**

What are the advantages and disadvantages of our energy resources?

A *A geothermal power station.*

Energy resource	Advantages	Disadvantages
geothermal	clean, cheap, renewable	It is only possible in certain parts of the world where hot rocks are near the surface of the Earth.
burning fossil fuels	cheap	non-renewable It produces carbon dioxide which causes global warming.
nuclear	It does not produce harmful gases.	expensive, non-renewable It produces dangerous radioactive substances that are difficult to get rid of.
solar	clean, renewable	No electricity is produced at night or if there is little sun. Solar panels do not collect very much heat energy. Solar cells are expensive and take up a lot of space.
hydroelectric	clean, renewable	Reservoirs take up huge amounts of space and destroy countryside. It only works in wet mountain regions.
wind	clean, renewable	Electricity is not produced if there is no wind. Wind turbines are noisy and many of them are needed to make useful amounts of electricity. Some people think that they spoil the countryside.
wave	clean, renewable	It does not produce very much electricity. It will not work in calm waters.
tidal	clean, renewable	It only works on some rivers. Dams across the rivers can affect wildlife. Tidal generators at sea could affect fish or shipping.
biomass	renewable It adds less carbon dioxide to the atmosphere than burning fossil fuels.	It may still add some carbon dioxide to the atmosphere. It needs large areas of land to grow crops.

1 Which of the renewable energy resources would be best to use in your area? Explain why. **H S W**

2 Which of the renewable energy resources would be useless in your area? Explain why. **H S W**

3 It costs a lot to build nuclear or hydroelectric power stations. Which energy resources would be best for countries that do not have a lot of money?

4 Your next-door neighbours want to put a wind turbine on their roof. **H S W**
   a How could this affect you?
   b How could they use renewable energy resources in a way that would affect their neighbours less?

7ld Eat up!

How much energy do our bodies need?

Humans and other animals need energy to live. We need energy to help us to grow and repair our bodies, and to move and keep warm. Our bodies use food as a source of energy, and release carbon dioxide when we use the food.

The unit for measuring energy is the **joule (J)**. The amount of energy needed to lift an apple from the floor onto a table is about 1 J. Most foods contain a lot more energy than this, so we usually measure the energy in foods using **kilojoules (kJ)**. 1 kJ = 1000 J.

A

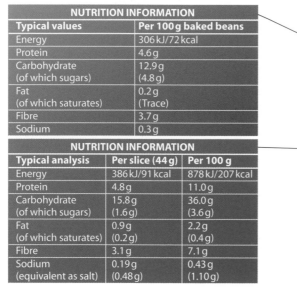

NUTRITION INFORMATION	
Typical values	**Per 100 g baked beans**
Energy	306 kJ/72 kcal
Protein	4.6 g
Carbohydrate (of which sugars)	12.9 g (4.8 g)
Fat (of which saturates)	0.2 g (Trace)
Fibre	3.7 g
Sodium	0.3 g

NUTRITION INFORMATION		
Typical analysis	**Per slice (44 g)**	**Per 100 g**
Energy	386 kJ/91 kcal	878 kJ/207 kcal
Protein	4.8 g	11.0 g
Carbohydrate (of which sugars)	15.8 g (1.6 g)	36.0 g (3.6 g)
Fat (of which saturates)	0.9 g (0.2 g)	2.2 g (0.4 g)
Fibre	3.1 g	7.1 g
Sodium (equivalent as salt)	0.19 g (0.48 g)	0.43 g (1.10 g)

B *Nutrition information for beans on toast.*

1 Why does your body need food?

2 a How much energy does 100 g of baked beans contain?

b Mark eats 200 g of baked beans on two slices of bread. How much energy is in the food he eats?

Ⓗ Ⓢ Ⓦ ⏳

The unit for measuring energy is named after James Joule (1818–1889) who was from Salford, England. Although he was a brewer, he did a lot of work on how energy was transferred from one form to another and how it was never destroyed. He told other scientists about his work at scientific meetings and by publishing scientific papers.

Ⓗ Ⓢ Ⓦ !

The old unit for measuring energy was the calorie. 1 calorie is about 4.2 joules.

Different people need different amounts of energy. Your body needs energy to help it to grow. If you do a lot of exercise, you need more energy than if you spend most of your time watching television.

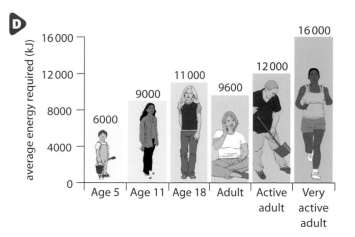

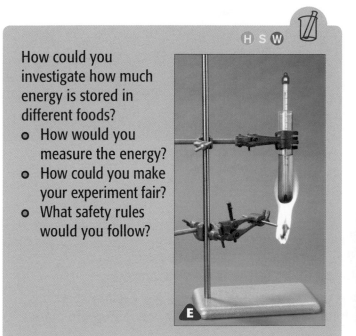

C *Mountaineers need to take their food with them when they climb mountains. They need to take food that will give them about 19 000 kJ per day.*

How could you investigate how much energy is stored in different foods?

- How would you measure the energy?
- How could you make your experiment fair?
- What safety rules would you follow?

Ⓗ Ⓢ Ⓦ

3 a Why does a teenager need more energy than a 5-year-old child?
  b Why do you think a pregnant woman needs more energy from food than one who is not pregnant?

4 a Write down these people in order of the energy they need, starting with the one who needs the least energy: baby, fire-fighter, secretary, 11-year-old child.
  b Explain your answer to part **a**.

5 a A 5-year-old only eats bread. How much would he have to eat each day to get the energy he needs?
  b If he only ate baked beans, how much would he have to eat each day?
  c Why shouldn't you try to eat just one type of food?

6 Scientists can measure the amount of energy stored in different foods. How can this knowledge help mountaineers and explorers? Ⓗ Ⓢ Ⓦ

I CAN...

- recall that our bodies need energy, which we get from food.
- explain why different people need different amounts of energy from food.
- recall that the units for measuring energy are joules (J) or kilojoules (kJ). 1 kJ = 1000 J. Ⓗ Ⓢ Ⓦ

The source is the Sun

Where does the energy originally come from?

Nearly all the energy stored in our energy resources originally came from the Sun. Heat and light from the Sun provide us with energy directly. Sunlight also provides the energy for plants to grow. The energy is needed for **photosynthesis**. This is the process where plants make their own food by using up carbon dioxide from the atmosphere. They convert carbon dioxide and water into glucose.

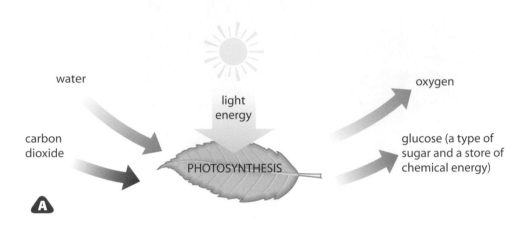

A

1 Where do plants get their energy from?
2 Where do animals get their energy from?

Coal, oil and natural gas were formed from the remains of dead plants and animals. The energy in these fuels came from the bodies of the plants and animals. The animals got their energy from the plants that they ate, and the plants got their energy from the Sun.

Solar power uses energy directly from the Sun. People in remote places use solar power for heating water and for making electricity. It is usually difficult to get electrical cables to these places. It is much easier and cheaper to use solar power.

B *Kamla runs a small factory in India that makes solar lighting systems. These panels supply electricity to the building, and need to be kept clean.*

3 What can people use solar power for?
4 a What are the advantages of using solar power?
　b What are the disadvantages of using solar power?
5 Bunsen burners use energy stored in natural gas. Explain where this energy came from originally, and how it came to be stored in the gas.

Solar power uses sunlight directly, but other energy resources also rely on the Sun. Wind is caused by the Sun heating up the Earth. We can see this most easily at the coast. Air above the land is heated up quickly. It rises and is replaced by colder air from the sea. This makes a wind called a **convection current**. The wind can turn wind turbines, and also makes the waves used in wave power.

Clouds form from water evaporated by the heat of the Sun. Eventually the water falls back to Earth as rain. Hydroelectric power therefore depends on the Sun.

Only three energy resources do not rely on the Sun. Nuclear power uses the nuclear energy stored in uranium, a metal found inside the Earth. **Tidal power** uses tides, caused by the gravity of the Moon. Geothermal power uses the heat from underground rocks.

Energy from the Sun can be used to power an aeroplane.

Energy from the wind can be used to generate electricity in remote locations.

6 Explain why wave power depends on the Sun.

7 Explain why hydroelectric power stations are not very useful in a drought.

8 The energy stored in a bowl of cornflakes and milk originally came from the Sun. Describe, without using a diagram, how the energy got into the cornflakes and milk.

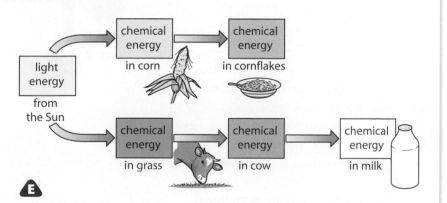

9 Unmuddle the names of these energy resources:
   i   A GERM HOTEL
   ii AN ULCER
   iii TRICYCLE HORDE
   For each one, say:
   a whether it depends on the Sun
   b whether it is renewable or non-renewable.

10 Design a poster to show the many ways that the Sun helps us to produce electricity. Ⓗ Ⓢ Ⓦ

I CAN...

o identify ways in which renewable energy resources can change people's lives. Ⓗ Ⓢ w

o explain that the Sun is the original source of energy for most of our energy resources.

o recall that the energy resources used in geothermal, tidal and nuclear power are the only ones that do not depend on the Sun.

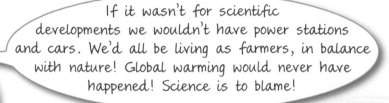

What has science got to do with global warming?

Most scientists think that burning fossil fuels is adding carbon dioxide to the atmosphere, and this is contributing to global warming. However not everyone agrees on the causes of global warming, or what we should be doing about it.

> If it wasn't for scientific developments we wouldn't have power stations and cars. We'd all be living as farmers, in balance with nature! Global warming would never have happened! Science is to blame!

A

> No-one knew about global warming when humans first started using fuels like coal. Scientists have discovered how our lifestyle is affecting the environment – now it's up to us to change the way we live.

B

> This concrete hides a generator powered by waves! Science and engineering can help us to find new ways of using renewable resources – we just need money for more research.

C

1 a Why do we need power stations?
  b How do power stations and cars contribute to global warming?
2 a Make a list of energy resources that do not contribute to global warming.
  b Why do you think that most of the electricity we use in this country still comes from non-renewable resources? Give as many reasons as you can.
3 a Why do you think many people do not want to change their lifestyles?
  b Suggest how people could be persuaded to make changes.

HAVE YOUR SAY

How have scientific ideas changed the way people live?
Is this a good thing?
What do you think?

Electricity

Electricity is a very useful way of moving energy from one place to another. Almost everything we do relies on electricity in some way.

All the electrical devices we use today depend on ideas developed by many different scientists. The first battery was made in 1794 by Alessandro Volta (1745–1827). Other scientists and inventors worked out how to measure current, and how to make light bulbs and motors. Computer chips weren't produced until 1971, so your grandparents would not have used many of the electrical things we use today.

Most of the large appliances in your home use **mains electricity**. Smaller items like MP3 players do not transfer as much energy, so they use **cells** (batteries) to provide electricity.

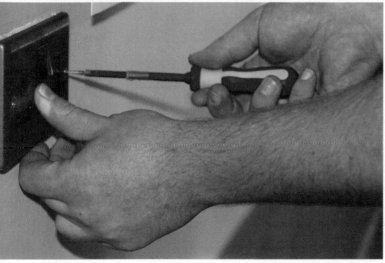

A *Houses are built with electrical wiring inside the walls, so that we can use electricity in all the rooms.*

B *Electricity is needed in the cars, the cameras and the timing equipment. Electricity was also used to make all these things.*

1 a Write down all the ways in which electricity is used in your home.
 b Which of the things in your list in part **a** could be done without electricity? (For example, you could cook using a gas cooker.)
 c Which things could not be done at all without electricity?
2 a What are the advantages of using cells in MP3 players and mobile phones?
 b What are the disadvantages?

How can we use electricity safely?

Electricity is very useful, but can also be very dangerous if it is not used properly.

Electricity experiments at school are safe because we use cells or **power packs** that provide a low **voltage**.

Lights use mains electricity, as do things like cookers and televisions. Mains electricity has a higher voltage than cells, so it can be dangerous.

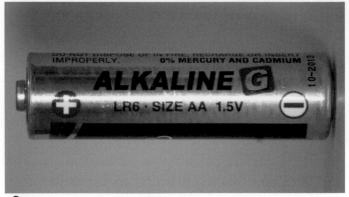

A One of these is called a **cell**. Cells contain a store of energy. When you use two or more together, it is called a **battery**.

General safety rules

- Never touch the bare metal parts of plugs.
- Never poke things into sockets.
- Keep electricity away from water.
- Do not plug too many things into one socket.
- Never use something that has a damaged wire.

Safety rules in science lessons

- Show your circuits to your teacher before switching them on.
- Never try to invent your own circuit.
- If you change your circuit, always switch the electricity off first.

Anything that uses electricity has to have:
- something to make the electricity flow (e.g. a cell)
- a complete **circuit** for the electricity to flow around.

The moving electricity is called an **electric current**.

A circuit is a complete loop that an electric current can flow around. If there is a gap in the circuit the current cannot flow.

1 Write down five things you should remember to stay safe when using electricity at home. **H S W**

2 Write down two things that you need to make something work using electricity.

We can control electricity using a switch. This switch is open, so there is a gap in the circuit and the current cannot flow.

When we close the switch there is a complete circuit for the current to flow around and the bulb lights up.

B

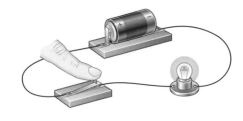

C

Electrical equipment is designed with safety in mind.

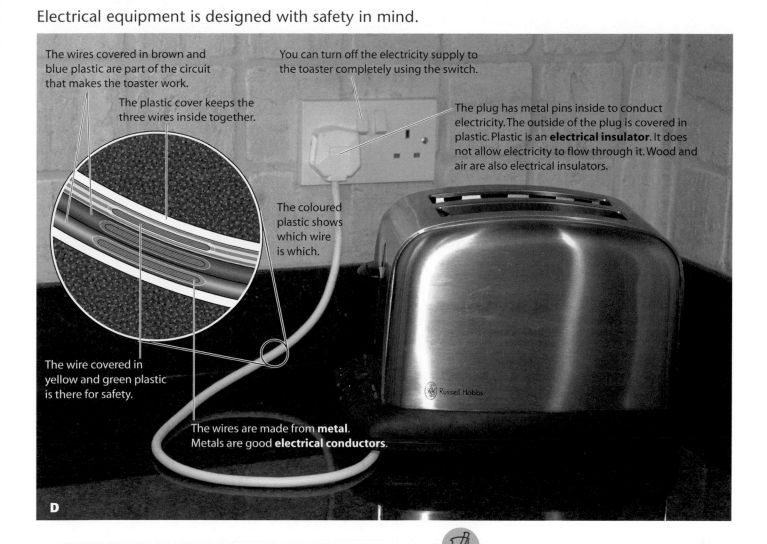

The wires covered in brown and blue plastic are part of the circuit that makes the toaster work.

The plastic cover keeps the three wires inside together.

You can turn off the electricity supply to the toaster completely using the switch.

The plug has metal pins inside to conduct electricity. The outside of the plug is covered in plastic. Plastic is an **electrical insulator**. It does not allow electricity to flow through it. Wood and air are also electrical insulators.

The coloured plastic shows which wire is which.

The wire covered in yellow and green plastic is there for safety.

The wires are made from **metal**. Metals are good **electrical conductors**.

D

How could you show that some materials conduct electricity and some do not?
o What apparatus and materials would you need?

E

3 Why are electrical wires made of metal?
4 Why are electrical wires usually covered in plastic?
5 Explain how a switch works. ⒽⓈⓌ
6 Design a poster to remind pupils how to use electricity safely at school. ⒽⓈⓌ

I **CAN...**

o recall the rules for using electricity safely. ⒽⓈⓌ
o explain what is needed to make an electric current flow.
o explain what electrical conductors and insulators are.

●●●**135**

How do we measure electricity?

The current is the amount of electricity that is flowing around a circuit. Bulbs light up because the current carries energy to the bulbs. A large current in a circuit makes bulbs bright. A small current makes them dim.

We measure the current using an **ammeter**. The units for current are **amps** (**A**).

An ammeter is put into a circuit like this:

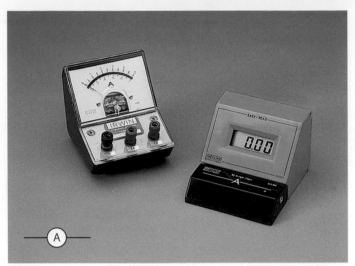

A *Different kinds of ammeter, and the symbol for an ammeter.*

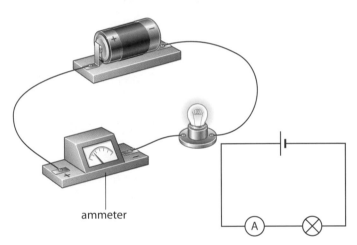

ammeter

B

It does not matter where the ammeter goes in the circuit. Current is not used up as it goes around the circuit, so the current is the same everywhere.

You can change the current in a circuit by changing the **components** in the circuit.

Circuit D has one bulb, and the current is 0.2 A.

André-Marie Ampère (1775–1836) was the first scientist to build a machine to measure the flow of electricity. He made many other discoveries about electricity, which he published in a scientific paper in 1826. The unit for current is named after him.

1 What does an ammeter measure?

2 Draw the symbol for an ammeter.

3 Look at circuit C.
  a What current will ammeter Y show?
  b What current will ammeter Z show?

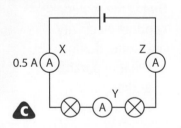

C

If you add another bulb, the current drops.

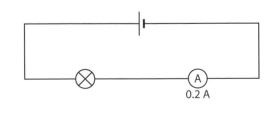

D

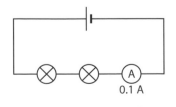

E

It is quite difficult for the current to flow through a circuit with a bulb in it. The current has to flow through a very thin piece of wire called the **filament**. If there are two bulbs in the circuit, it is even more difficult for the current to get around the circuit, so the current is smaller.

Components (including bulbs) which make it more difficult for a current to flow around a circuit have a high **resistance**. Components which do not make it difficult for the current to flow have a low resistance. Connecting wires have a low resistance.

Sometimes we only need a very small current in a circuit. We can make the current smaller by using a **resistor** in the circuit. A resistor has a high resistance and makes it harder for electricity to flow.

The current in a circuit can also be changed by changing the voltage. A cell has a voltage marked on it. Cells with high voltages will produce bigger currents. You can put cells together in a circuit to get a bigger voltage. The chemicals inside the cell provide the voltage.

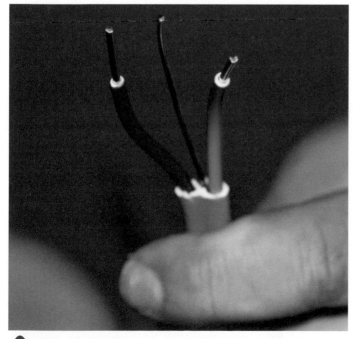

G *The wires in houses are very thick, so they have a very low resistance.*

4 Look at circuits D and E. (H)(S)(W)
  a Why is the current smaller in circuit E than in circuit D?
  b Which circuit will have the brightest bulbs? Explain your answer.
  c What would happen to the current if you put another bulb into circuit E?

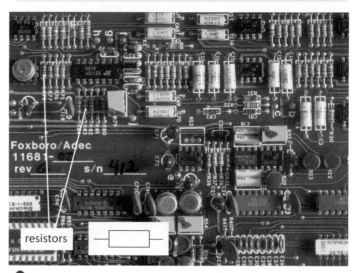

resistors

F *The symbol for a resistor and resistors on a circuit board.*

(H) S (W)

How can you find out how the current changes when you add more bulbs to a circuit?
  o What equipment would you need?

5 Why is it important for wiring in houses to have a low resistance?

6 A torch is not working. Write down all the things that could be wrong with it.

I CAN...

  o use an ammeter. (H)(S)w
  o explain that resistance is a way of saying how easy it is for current to flow through something.
  o describe some ways of changing the current in a circuit.

How do we use electricity?

When a current flows through a wire, the wire may get hot. The heat produced by electricity can be useful.

Electricity is used to heat the blade of the knife in photo A, so it can cut through materials such as plastic or rubber.

If a piece of metal gets hot enough it gives out light as well as heat. Light bulbs have a piece of wire, called the filament, inside the glass. The filament has a high resistance. When a current flows through the filament, it gets so hot that it glows.

A

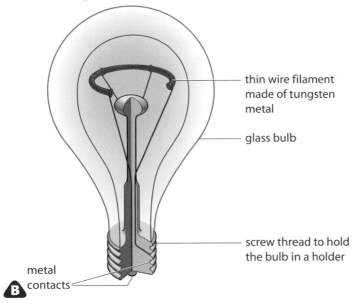

thin wire filament made of tungsten metal

glass bulb

screw thread to hold the bulb in a holder

metal contacts

B

H S W

How could you find out whether a long wire or a short wire has the highest resistance?
- What equipment would you need?
- How would you stay safe?

H S W

Thomas Edison (1847–1931) is often given credit for inventing the light bulb. However, several other people had worked on developing light bulbs, and patented their ideas. A patent gives the person the right to make money out of their invention. Joseph Swan (1828–1914) had an earlier patent on light bulbs. Eventually the two men formed a joint company to sell the bulbs.

1 What happens to the temperature of a wire when a current flows through it?

2 Write a list of all the appliances you can think of that heat up when electricity flows through them.

If a piece of metal gets too hot, it may melt. The steel wool in photo C conducts electricity. If the current is increased, the steel wool glows. If the current is increased even more, the steel wool will melt.

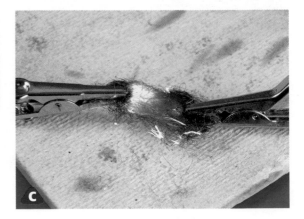
C

A **fuse** is a piece of wire that is designed to melt if the current gets too big.

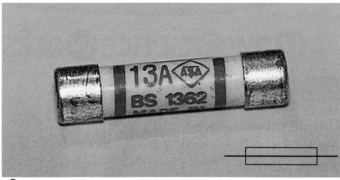

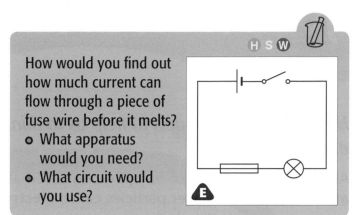

How would you find out how much current can flow through a piece of fuse wire before it melts?
o What apparatus would you need?
o What circuit would you use?

D A fuse and the symbol for a fuse.

For most pieces of electrical equipment, the fuse is in the plug. If an appliance, like an iron, goes wrong a lot of electricity may flow through the wires. This can make the wires in the walls of the house very hot and make them catch fire. The plug has a fuse in it to stop this happening. The high current makes the fuse melt, so no more current can flow. It is important to have the correct fuse fitted in a plug. All appliances have a label on them to show what fuse should be used.

Equipment	Fuse
kettle	13 A
iron	13 A
TV	5 A
music centre	5 A
DVD player	3 A
central heating pump	3 A

G Fuses used in some common appliances.

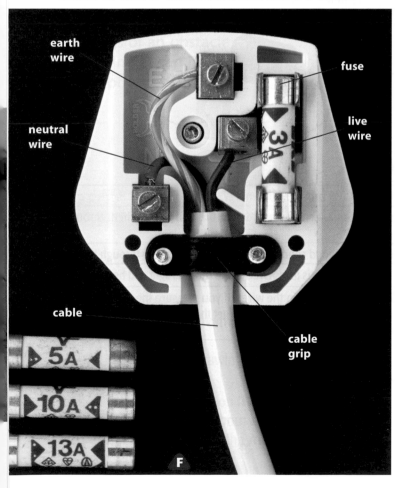

F

3 How does a fuse stop the current flowing if the current is too big?

4 How can a fuse protect electrical equipment?

5 Which pieces of equipment in table G use the most current? Explain how you worked out your answer.

6 What do you think would happen if you put a:
   a 3 A fuse in a plug used for a kettle Ⓗ Ⓢ Ⓦ
   b 13 A fuse in a plug used for a TV? Ⓗ Ⓢ Ⓦ

I CAN...

o recall that some wires get hot when a current flows through them.
o explain what a fuse does.
o choose the correct fuse for an appliance. Ⓗ Ⓢ w

How do our bodies use electricity?

When you move, your brain sends electrical signals, called **impulses**, to your muscles. These impulses travel along your **nerves**. Your nerves are not made out of metal, and electricity does not travel through them in the same way as it does through a wire.

One of the most important muscles in your body is your heart. Your heart can only pump blood properly if the different parts of it move at the right times. The heart muscle is controlled by electrical impulses, just like all the other muscles in your body.

Sometimes the impulses cannot reach all parts of the heart properly. When this happens, doctors can fit a pacemaker. A small electrical cell is put just under the skin, and a very thin wire goes into the heart. This carries impulses to the muscles at the right times.

If a patient's heart has stopped beating, it can sometimes be made to start again by passing electricity through it. The machine that does this is called a defibrillator.

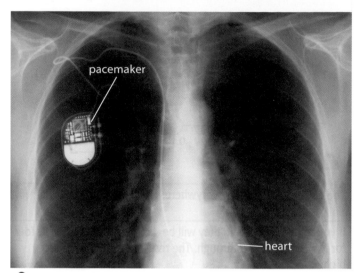

A An X-ray of a person's chest. A pacemaker has been fitted.

1 a Which cells carry electricity around your body?
  b How do these cells help the body?
2 How can modern technology help some people with heart problems? **H** **S** **W**

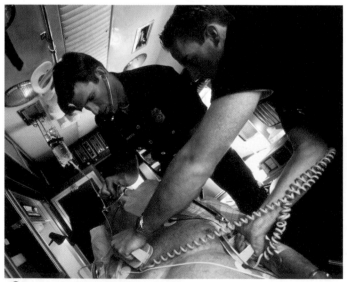

B A defibrillator being used.

Some animals can make electricity in their bodies. An electric eel can give a shock of 1000 volts.

Our bodies use electricity, but electricity can also harm us. An **electric shock** can burn the skin, or can stop our nerves working properly. Electric shocks can kill people by upsetting the nerves that control their hearts, or the nerves that control their breathing.

Table D shows the effects of different currents on a human body.

Current	Effect
0.001 A	This current can be felt.
0.005 A	This amount of current is painful.
0.010 A	This current can make muscles contract.
0.015 A	You cannot control your muscles if there is this current flowing through your body.
0.070 A	This current can kill you.

D

Your body has a much higher resistance than a component like a light bulb. That is why you do not usually feel anything if you accidentally touch a 12 V circuit in a school experiment. However, mains electricity at 230 V will give you a nasty shock.

E This electric fence is used to stop horses getting into the wrong field. The horses get a small electric shock if they touch it, so they do not try to push it over.

F This electrical equipment is at a very high voltage. You could be killed if you touch it.

The resistance of your skin is much lower when it is wet, so a much higher current would flow through you. This is why it is so dangerous to use switches or other electrical equipment with wet hands. Light switches in bathrooms are fitted in the ceiling so that you cannot touch them with wet hands. You have to pull a long cord to turn the switch on or off. Electricians are not allowed to put sockets in bathrooms.

3 You might have a current of 0.2 A flowing in a circuit you use at school, but if you accidentally touch the bare wires you do not usually feel a shock. Why not? (*Hint:* think about the resistance of a bulb compared to the resistance of your body.)

H S W !

People sweat very slightly when they are telling lies. This makes their skin wetter and changes its resistance. Lie detectors measure the resistance of the skin and show when someone is lying. Unfortunately these detectors are not very reliable!

4 Describe two ways in which an electric shock could kill you.

5 How can electric shocks be useful? Think of as many ways as you can. H S W

6 Why is it dangerous to use electrical equipment with wet hands? Explain in as much detail as you can. H S W

I CAN...

o recall that nerves carry electrical impulses around the body.

o describe ways in which electricity can help or harm the body.

How did scientists find out about electricity?

HowScienceWorks

Many scientists have studied electricity and carried out experiments to find out more about it. However, scientists do not always agree on what the results of an experiment mean.

Dr Luigi Galvani (1737–1798) studied how muscles work at the University of Bologna in Italy in the 1780s. One day he was examining a nerve in a frog's leg. He noticed that it twitched when a spark was made by a machine at the other end of the laboratory.

Galvani thought that the twitch was connected with the spark. He predicted that other sparks of electricity should make a frog's leg twitch. He tested this idea by hanging a frog's leg outside when there was a thunderstorm. The leg twitched when lightning flashed.

Unfortunately for Galvani's theory, he also found that he could get a frog's leg to twitch without lightning. The leg would twitch if he pushed a copper hook into a frog's nerve and hung it on an iron wire.

Galvani decided that animals' bodies contained a new kind of electricity, which he called 'animal electricity'. He thought that this animal electricity would make muscles twitch when a piece of metal connected the nerve to the muscles. He published his findings in a paper in 1791.

1 Write down three ways in which Galvani could make the frogs' legs twitch.
2 Why did Galvani think that the frogs' legs were making 'animal electricity'?

A Lightning is a form of electricity.

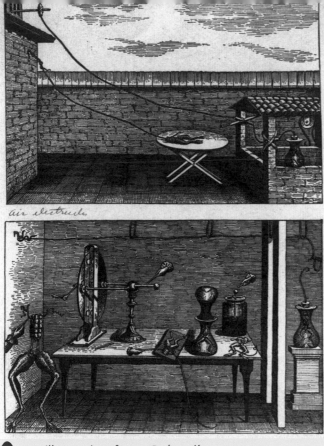

B *An illustration from Galvani's paper.*

Alessandro Volta (1745–1827) was a professor of physics at the University of Pavia, in Italy. Volta read about Galvani's experiments with frogs' legs and tried the experiments for himself. He got similar results, but did not believe that the frog's leg had produced the electricity. He thought that the two metals, copper and iron, had made the electricity when they touched. He believed that the electricity made by the metals had made the leg twitch.

3 a How did Volta find out about Galvani's ideas?
  b Suggest how scientists find out about each other's ideas today.
4 What did Volta think about:
  a the results of Galvani's experiments
  b the conclusion that Galvani drew from his results?

In 1794, Volta started experimenting to test his theory by trying to make electricity without any animal tissue. Eventually, Volta made a cell from a pile of pieces of zinc and copper, with each pair of metals separated by paper soaked in salty water.

In 1800, he wrote to the Royal Society in London (a scientific organisation) to tell them about his discovery. In 1801, the Emperor Napoleon summoned him to Paris to demonstrate his cell. Volta's work was so important that his name was used as the unit for measuring the energy carried by electricity, the volt.

5 How did Volta show that Galvani's ideas about animal electricity were wrong?
6 Why is it important for scientists to communicate their ideas and results?

Volta and Galvani were both partly right and partly wrong. Galvani was correct, because we now know that nerves do conduct electricity, but it is not a different kind of electricity. Volta was also correct – electricity can be produced by the contact between two different metals (although this is not the way electricity is produced in our bodies).

C *Volta demonstrating his pile.*

HowScienceWorks

Should we use electric cars?

In many places, milk used to be delivered every day. The deliveries were usually very early, so that people had milk in time for breakfast. The milk floats usually had electric motors, using energy stored in a battery. The motors were quiet, produced no pollution and were better at stopping and starting frequently than petrol engines.

Today, some new cars use electric motors running from batteries instead of petrol engines. New cars are being developed that use fuel cells, which combine oxygen and hydrogen gases to make electricity. The only waste from a fuel cell is water vapour.

A

Electric cars cut down pollution in cities and make the roads quieter.

But they can't go very far before you need to recharge the battery. And they only move the pollution from the city to the countryside.

Ben   **Sue**

B

1 Write a list of all the things that electricity can be used for in a car.

2 Why were electric motors used in milk floats? Give as many reasons as you can.

3 What do you think Sue means by saying that electric cars 'only move the pollution'? (*Hint*: think about where the electricity to recharge the battery comes from.)

4 a Why do you think most cars still use petrol or diesel engines?
   b What could the government do to persuade more people to use electric cars?

HAVE YOUR SAY

Are electric cars a good thing? Should everyone be using electric cars? What do you think?

Sports and forces

Our life is full of **forces**. We cannot see them but we can see how they affect things. All sports involve forces. You use a force when you kick a football, when you ride a bike, or when you run.

When you take part in certain sports you need special equipment to protect you from some forces, or to help you to produce bigger forces. Many sports would not be possible without modern technology.

A *New designs of ropes and other climbing equipment mean that more people can climb safely. The ropes will stop the climbers hitting the ground if they fall off the rock. They wear special shoes to increase the force of* **friction** *between their feet and the rock.*

B *Forces from the engine and the wings allow the aeroplane to fly. The skydivers will open their parachutes when they get near to the ground, and the force of* **air resistance** *will slow them down.*

The first freefall jump from an aeroplane was made in 1914.

C *The kayak has to provide enough* **upthrust** *to stay on top of the water. It has a smooth shape to reduce its* **water resistance**.

1 Write down five sports which you can play using only simple equipment such as a ball.
2 Look at the photos on this page. Which sports could have been played 200 years ago? Explain your answer.
3 Climbers can now climb much steeper rock faces than they could 50 years ago. Suggest why this is.
4 Write down five sports which you could not do without modern technology.

7Ka The forces are with us

What can forces do?

Forces can change the shape of something, its speed, or the direction that it is moving in.

1 Write down three ways in which a force can affect an object.

Many forces need to touch an object before they can affect it. These are called **contact forces**. For example, when you throw a ball, you need to touch the ball to put a force on it. When you go down a steep hill on a bicycle, the brakes need to touch the wheel to produce friction to slow you down.

Some forces can affect an object from a distance. These are called **non-contact forces**.

A

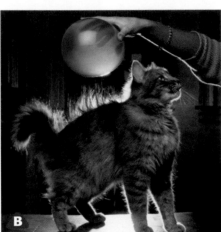

B

C

Any two objects have a force of attraction between them. This force is called **gravity**. The Earth is so big that its gravity is very strong, and pulls us all towards it.

Static electricity can attract charged things.

This model is held together by magnets. Magnets have **magnetism**, which attracts objects made of iron.

2 Write down the names of three non-contact forces.

Sometimes there are a lot of forces acting on something. There are four forces acting on the diver in photo D.

We can use arrows to show forces. The direction of the arrow shows the direction of the force, and a bigger arrow shows a bigger force.

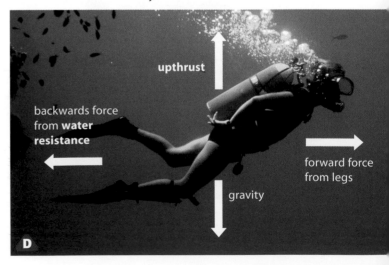

upthrust

backwards force from **water resistance**

forward force from legs

gravity

D

We measure forces using a **force meter** (also known as a **newton meter**). A force meter has a spring inside it which can be stretched. The amount of stretch in the spring depends on the size of the force. The units for measuring forces are **newtons** (N).

Your **weight** is the force of gravity pulling on you. Weight is a force, so its units are newtons (N). If you talk about something being '10 kilograms' you are talking about its **mass**. Weight and mass are two different things.

Mass is the amount of matter which makes something up. The units for measuring mass are **grams** (g) and **kilograms** (kg).

On Earth, gravity pulls on every kilogram with a force of 10 N. If a bag of apples has a mass of 2 kg, its weight on Earth will be 20 N (multiply 2 kg by 10). If you went to the Moon, where the gravity is not as strong, its mass would still be 2 kg but its weight would only be about 3 N. The gravity on the Moon is only one sixth as strong as it is on Earth.

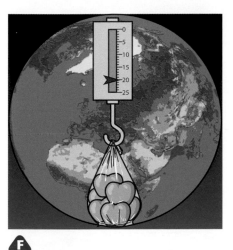

F

3 What do we use to measure forces?
4 What are the units for measuring forces?

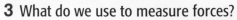 **H S W**

The 'true' kilogram mass is kept in a safe near Paris. All other kilogram masses are measured against this one.

E

5 a What is weight?
  b What are the units for weight?
6 Why would you weigh less on the Moon than you do on the Earth?
7 What are the units for measuring mass?
8 Why do you think it is important that scientists in different countries all check their ways of measuring a kilogram against the same standard mass? **H S W**

I CAN...

○ describe what forces can do.
○ recall the names of the contact and non-contact forces.
○ explain how to measure forces.
○ explain the difference between weight and mass.

7Kb Friction

How can we control friction?

Friction is the force between two touching objects. It can slow things down or make things stay still. The friction between your clothes and a chair stops you from sliding off it. Walking would be very difficult without the friction between your feet and the floor – you would slip and slide everywhere.

We can increase friction by using certain materials. Rubber produces a lot of friction. For example, the tyres of a Formula One racing car stop the car from sliding off the road as it speeds round a sharp bend.

1 Give one example of friction making something stay still.
2 Explain why rubber bath mats are useful. **H S W**

A *Rock climbing shoes are made from special rubber that increases friction and gives a good grip.*

B *Friction keeps knots done up, and helps the climber to control the rope.*

H S W

What factors affect the amount of friction?
- Which factors could you test?
- How can you make your test fair?

Friction is not always useful. Sometimes we want things to move easily. For example, a bicycle is very difficult to ride if there is too much friction in the axles. We can reduce friction by making surfaces smooth, or by using **lubricants** such as oil or grease. Adding a lubricant is called **lubrication**.

Skiers wax the bottom of their skis to make them very smooth. This reduces friction and allows them to ski faster. **C**

> The first speed skiing record was set in 1874, when Tommy Todd reached a speed of nearly 141 km/h (88 mph). The current record is over 250 km/h (155 mph).

Friction can also wear things away. The brake pads on a bicycle eventually wear away, and so do car tyres. Parts of your clothes get thinner as friction wears them away.

Friction produces heat and noise. If a car engine runs without any oil in it, the large friction between the moving parts causes it to overheat and stop working. Rusty door hinges squeak and make a door difficult to open.

Gases and liquids can also cause friction. **Air resistance** and water resistance are both kinds of friction. These kinds of friction can be reduced by having smooth surfaces and smooth shapes.

3 a Why should you oil the axles of a bicycle?
  b Why must you never put oil on the brake blocks of a bicycle?
  c Explain why bicycle brakes do not work very well in the rain.
4 Why do you think the speed skiing record has increased by over 100 km/h since 1874? **H S W**

D *The hang glider pilot has a low air resistance because the air can move smoothly over her body.*

5 Why do car owners have to replace their car tyres regularly?
6 How could you stop a door hinge squeaking?
7 Write down three things that friction can do to a moving object.
8 Describe as many ways as you can in which friction is useful to you in your everyday life.
9 Write a diary entry for 'The day friction disappeared'.

I CAN...

- explain when friction is useful and when it is not useful.
- describe how to increase friction.
- describe how to reduce friction.

Why do some things float and some things sink?

When you are standing on the ground, gravity is pulling you down. An upwards force from the ground stops you sinking into the Earth.

When you float in water, you feel that you weigh less. This is because there is a force from the water called upthrust. This pushes up against your weight. You still have weight, but you do not feel it. An object will float when the upthrust cancels out its weight.

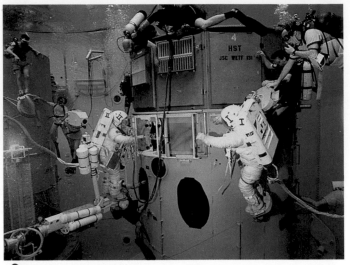

A Astronauts train in a big tank of water. This gives them the same 'weightless' feeling that they will get in space.

B

1 a What two forces affect you when you float?
   b How do these two forces compare in size?

2 A boy's weight is 500 N. What upthrust does he need to float?

3 A hot air balloon is floating in the air. The air gives upthrust.
   a What are the two forces acting on it?
   b What can you say about the sizes of the two forces?

You can work out if something will float if you know its **density**. Density measures how much mass there is in 1 cm³ of something. The density of an object is worked out by finding its mass and dividing by its volume. You can use this formula:

$$\text{density} = \frac{\text{mass}}{\text{volume}}$$

To work out density you must make sure that you have measured the mass in grams and the volume in cm³.

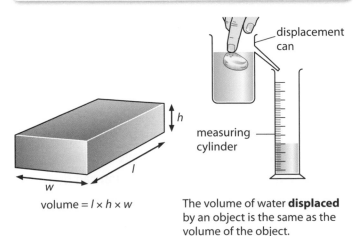

volume = $l \times h \times w$

The volume of water **displaced** by an object is the same as the volume of the object.

C There are two ways of finding the volume of an object.

The density of water is 1g/cm³. If something has a density less than 1g/cm³ it will float in water.

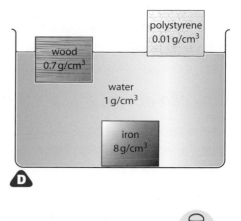

D

polystyrene
0.01 g/cm³

wood
0.7 g/cm³

water
1 g/cm³

iron
8 g/cm³

H S W

How can you measure the upthrust when an object is put into water?
o How can you predict whether or not the object will float?
o How could you find out if the type of liquid makes a difference to the upthrust?

E

Mercury is a metal that is liquid at room temperature. Its density is much greater than the density of water. Things can float in it very easily.

This photograph F *was taken in 1972. This would not be allowed today, as mercury is toxic (poisonous).*

H S W

Ideas about density were first used to catch a thief! Archimedes (287–212 BCE) was an inventor who lived in Sicily. The king of Sicily had given some gold to a metal worker to be made into a crown, but he thought that the man was stealing some of the gold and mixing silver with it instead. Archimedes worked out the density of pure gold and compared it with the density of the crown. The densities were different, so he had proved that the man was cheating.

4 a Copy and complete this table.

Material	Mass (g)	Volume (cm³)	Density (g/cm³)	Float or sink in water?
W	40	10		
X	50	100		
Y	80	20		
Z	200	250		

b Which two materials could be the same? Explain your answer. H S W

5 Why do you think that pregnant women often find it easier to exercise in a swimming pool?

6 Suggest how Archimedes might have measured the volume of the crown. H S W

7 Steel is denser than water, so how can a steel ship float? (*Hint*: think about what is inside the ship.) H S W

I CAN...
o explain what upthrust means.
o calculate the density of a material. H S W

●●● 155

How can adventure sports be safe?

Some sports are more dangerous than others. You are more likely to have a serious accident if you go rock climbing or kayaking than if you play football or take part in athletics. But adventure sports are becoming more and more popular because modern equipment can make them safer.

Rock climbers use ropes and other equipment so that if they fall off a mountain, they do not fall very far. The equipment they use is made just for rock climbing, and the manufacturers test it all carefully to make sure it is strong enough for its purpose. Climbers also check their equipment before using it, to make sure it has not been damaged. It isn't enough just to have the right equipment. You must also know how to use it properly.

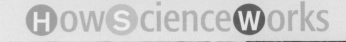

The helmet protects the climber's head from falling stones, or if he falls and hits his head on the rock.

The rope stops him falling if he cannot hold onto the rock.

The harness is attached to the rope. It spreads his weight around his legs if he is hanging on the rope, so the rope does not cut into his waist or chest.

A

The rope must be tied to the harness with a special knot that will not slip if there is a big force on the rope.

The belt of the harness must be fastened correctly to make sure it does not come undone.

B

The rope is holding the climber to the rock.

If the climber falls, ther be a sudden, large forc the rope. The belay dev helps this climber to ho onto the rope even if t is a big force on it. The must be threaded thro the belay device prope

The belay devic is fastened to th harness with a karabiner. This s makes sure the karabiner cann come undone.

C

1 Why do rock climbers:
   a use ropes
   b need to wear helmets
   c need harnesses?

2 How could a manufacturer test the following types of equipment to make sure they were suitable for use in climbing?
   a rope   b helmet   c harness

3 Rock climbers look after their ropes carefully. What could happen if a rope was damaged?

4 Look carefully at the buckle on the harness in photo B. How is the way it is fastened different to the way a normal belt is fastened? Suggest why it is fastened this way.

5 Look at photo C.
   a Why is the climber fastened to the rock? Use the word 'force' in your answer.
   b What could happen if the climber had not fastened herself to the rock properly?

People who run factories or laboratories and schools must carry out **risk assessments**, to make sure that the activities that go on there will be as safe as possible. Outdoor centres also do risk assessments for activities such as rock climbing.

A risk assessment first considers all the possible **hazards** (dangers) that could occur, how likely each hazard is to occur, and how serious the results would be if it did happen. This gives the risk.

People who do adventure sports do not normally write out risk assessments, but they have usually thought about them before they set off.

D

Hazard – I might fall off, and I would be hurt if I hit the ground. How likely? – quite likely to happen as this is a hard route for me. Seriousness – I have all the right equipment, and I know how to use it. I will check all my equipment for damage before I start. If I do fall off I am not likely to hit the ground. Risk – low. Let's go climbing!

6 What is the difference between a hazard and a risk?

7 Write down some hazards that exist for the following activities. For each one, say how serious the consequences could be, and how the risk could be kept as low as possible.
   a Going on a long walk in the mountains, where you will be miles from the nearest road.
   b Kayaking to an island 10 miles from the coast.

What happens when forces are balanced?

Forces can add together. It is difficult for one person to push a broken down car. If another person helps, it is easier to push the car because their forces are added together.

Two forces can also work against each other if they are in opposite directions. If the two forces are the same size, nothing will happen. The forces are **balanced**.

If one of the forces is stronger than the other, something will start to move. The forces are **unbalanced**.

All **stationary** (still) objects have balanced forces on them. Moving objects can also have balanced forces on them. If the forces are balanced the object carries on moving at the same speed. The speed only changes when the forces are unbalanced.

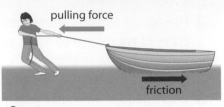

A *The forces on the boat are balanced.*

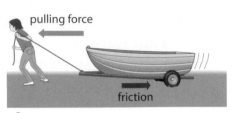

B *Unbalanced forces.*

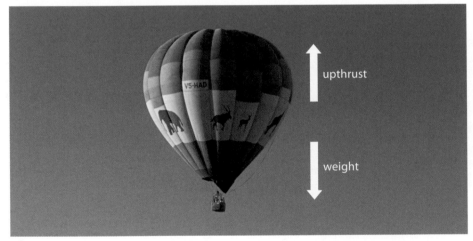

C *This balloon is not moving because its weight is being balanced by the upthrust.*

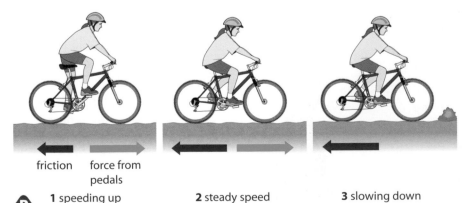

friction   force from pedals

D   **1** speeding up   **2** steady speed   **3** slowing down

1 Look at pictures A and B.
 a Why isn't the boat moving in A?
 b Why is the boat moving in B?

2 Look at photo C. What will happen if the pilot increases the amount of upthrust from the balloon? Explain your answer.

3 Look at drawing D. Why is the girl:
 a speeding up in 1
 b going at a steady speed in 2
 c slowing down in 3?

A force meter can be used to measure a force because the spring inside it stretches when it is pulled. The spring is **elastic** because it goes back to its original shape after it has been stretched. Plasticine® will also stretch but it is not elastic.

Robert Hooke (1635–1703) was a famous British scientist who studied how metals behave when they stretch. His work led to the invention of the force meter. However, the units for measuring forces were named after his rival and arch enemy, Isaac Newton!

When you first hang something on a force meter, the forces are not balanced, so the spring begins to stretch.

As the spring stretches, it produces a bigger force.

Eventually the forces are balanced. The force meter is showing the weight of the object.

E

4 What does weight mean?

5 Graph F shows how far different materials stretch when a weight is hung on them. Ⓗ Ⓢ Ⓦ

a Which material stretches the most for a certain weight?

b Which two materials could be used for making a force meter? Explain your answer.

c Which material would be best for making a force meter to measure small weights?

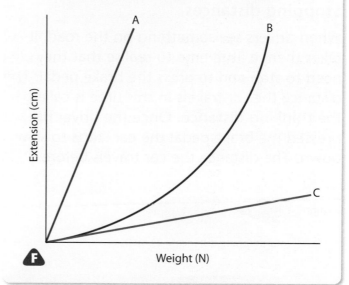

F Weight (N)

How could you make your own force meter?

○ What elastic object will you use?

○ How would you find out how much it stretches with different weights?

○ How would you use it to weigh an object?

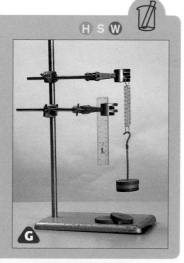

G

I CAN...

○ explain what happens to stationary and moving objects when the forces on them are balanced.

○ explain how a force meter works.

○ use a force meter.

Ⓗ Ⓢ w

How can we show how fast something is moving?

Speed is a way of saying how far you travel in a certain time. This time can be a second (s), a minute (min) or an hour (h) or even longer.

To work out a speed, you have to measure a distance and a time. The units you use for speed depend on the measurements you take. For instance, if a car travels 200 miles in 4 hours, its speed would be in **miles per hour** (mph). Other units for speed that are often used are **kilometres per hour** (km/h) and **metres per second** (m/s).

> **1** A bus travelled 60 km in 2 hours. What units would you use for its speed?
>
> **2** You are growing a little taller each year. What units could you use to measure how fast you are growing?

Stopping distances

When drivers see something on the road, it takes them a little time to realise that they need to stop and to press the brake pedal. The distance the car travels in this time is called the **thinking distance**. Once the driver has pressed the brake pedal the car starts to slow down. The distance the car travels before it stops is called the **braking distance**. The total distance the car moves is called the **stopping distance**. The faster a car is going, the longer it takes to stop.

The distances in the diagram are based on measurements made with a family car that is working properly, with good tyres, on a dry road.

■ thinking distance

■ braking distance

30 mph | 9 m | 14 m

total stopping distance = 23 m

70 mph | 21 m | 75 m

A total stopping distance = 96 m

> **3 a** What will happen to the braking distance if the road is wet?
>
> **b** Why will this happen?
>
> **c** What should drivers do on wet roads?

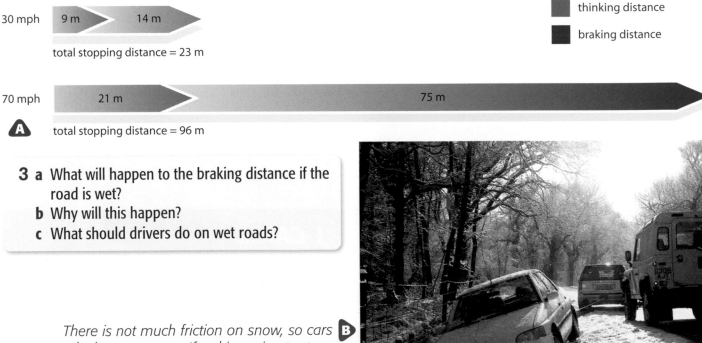

There is not much friction on snow, so cars **B** *take longer to stop. If a driver tries to stop or turn too suddenly, the car may skid.*

Distance–time graphs

You can show how fast someone travelled during a journey by using a **distance–time graph**. This graph shows Jenny's day out on her bicycle.

A steep line on a distance–time graph shows that something is moving quickly. A shallow line shows it is moving slowly. If the line is horizontal it is not moving at all.

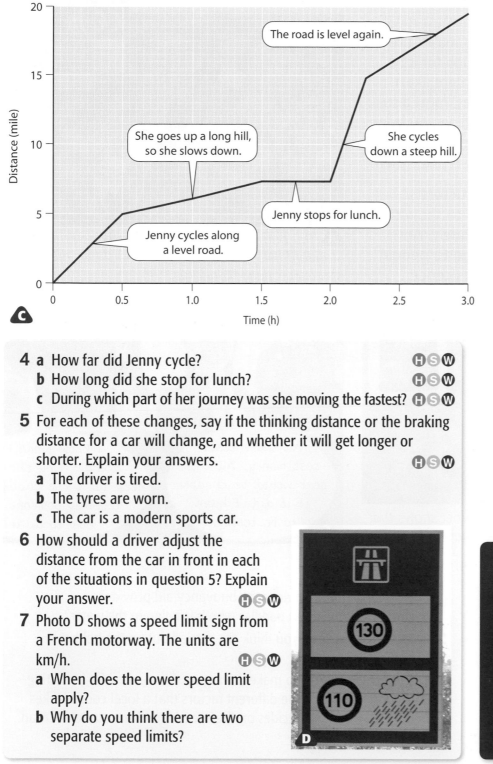

4 **a** How far did Jenny cycle? ⒽⓈⓌ
  b How long did she stop for lunch? ⒽⓈⓌ
  c During which part of her journey was she moving the fastest? ⒽⓈⓌ

5 For each of these changes, say if the thinking distance or the braking distance for a car will change, and whether it will get longer or shorter. Explain your answers. ⒽⓈⓌ
  a The driver is tired.
  b The tyres are worn.
  c The car is a modern sports car.

6 How should a driver adjust the distance from the car in front in each of the situations in question 5? Explain your answer. ⒽⓈⓌ

7 Photo D shows a speed limit sign from a French motorway. The units are km/h. ⒽⓈⓌ
  a When does the lower speed limit apply?
  b Why do you think there are two separate speed limits?

I CAN...

○ recall the different units used to measure speed. ⒽⓈw

○ explain that cars take longer to stop if they are travelling faster.

○ interpret distance–time graphs. ⒽⓈw

HowScienceWorks

Why do we need safety standards for sports?

All equipment for adventure sports must meet certain standards. These standards make sure that the equipment is strong enough for its purpose, and is safe to use. Equipment like a climbing helmet, or climbing ropes, must also be sold with instruction leaflets telling you how to use them properly, how to look after them, and how to tell when you need to replace them.

There are also standards for instructors. Instructors can get qualifications to show that they know how to teach others safely. Any outdoor centres that offer training to people under the age of 18 must have a licence.

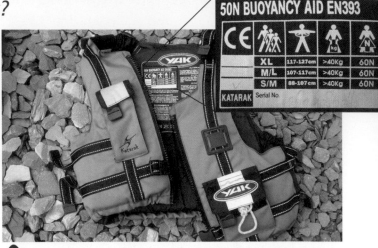

A *This buoyancy aid has been tested to European Standard EN393. The CE mark also shows that it meets European standards.*

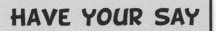

B *The CE label on this climbing helmet shows that it meets European Standards. The label inside states which US standards it meets.*

All those tests cost money. All this gear would be cheaper if it didn't have to be tested.

I know what I'm doing – why should I need all those qualifications to show someone else how to do it?

HAVE YOUR SAY

Some people think that there are too many rules and regulations. Do you think there should be standards for equipment and for instructors?

1 Look at photo A.
  a How much upthrust does the buoyancy aid provide?
  b How does this help a paddler who has fallen in the water?

2 What kinds of test do you think are carried out on the helmet in photo B?

3 The government tries to make driving on the roads safer by setting speed limits. Suggest the different factors that a local council takes into account when it decides on the speed limit for a stretch of road. Explain your answer.

Observing the sky

HowScienceWorks

All life on **Earth** depends on the **Sun**. The Sun appears to move across the sky each day. The way it moves is different in summer and winter.

People have always been able to see that the Sun appears to move across the sky. Observations of the Sun and the stars have been recorded for over 5000 years. They were used to help people to work out a calendar, so that farmers knew when to plant crops.

Most ancient peoples also believed that the stars and the Sun were connected to the Gods, or could foretell the future. Many observations were used for religious reasons.

A The Sun is essential for life on Earth.

C **Astronomers** are scientists who study the stars. These are amateur astronomers observing the moon.

B Stonehenge is believed to be over 5000 years old. The rising Sun in the middle of summer shines between the most important stones.

Ancient people had no instruments such as telescopes to help them to make their observations. Today, almost anyone can make accurate observations of the stars using binoculars or telescopes.

Warning: never look directly at the Sun – it could damage your eyes.

1 a Why did some ancient people make observations of the Sun and the stars?
 b Why do you think that astronomers study the stars today?

2 Think about your own observations of the Sun and the Moon.
 a How does the Sun appear to move across the sky during the day?
 b What are the differences in the way the Sun moves between summer and winter?
 c Describe how the shape of the Moon seems to change during a month.

7La A place near the Sun

How can we explain days, nights and years?

Scientists work out ideas and **models** to explain observations. There have been many different ideas about why we have days, nights and years. The model explained here is a set of ideas that was worked out nearly 500 years ago, although some of the ideas are much older than that. This is the model that all scientists today think is correct.

We live on a **planet** called **Earth**. The Earth is shaped like a **sphere**. The Earth gets heat and light from the **Sun**.

Day and night

The Earth spins on its **axis**. A **day** in **astronomy** is the time it takes for a planet to make one complete spin. It takes 24 hours for this to happen on Earth.

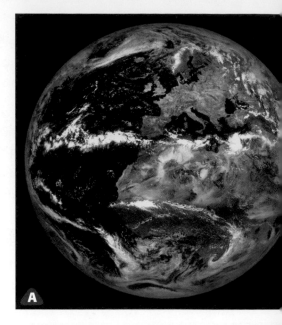

A

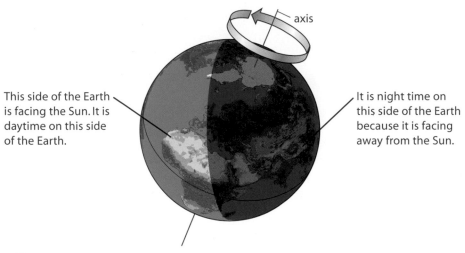

This side of the Earth is facing the Sun. It is daytime on this side of the Earth.

It is night time on this side of the Earth because it is facing away from the Sun.

axis

B

The Sun seems to move across the sky during the day. It rises in the east and sets in the west. This happens because the Earth is spinning, *not* because the Sun is moving around the Earth.

C *The bright line shows how the Sun moves across the sky on a winter's day in Finland.*

1 What provides the Earth with heat and light?
2 How long does it take the Earth to spin once round its axis?
3 Use the model shown in diagram B to explain why shadows move during the day. Ⓗ Ⓢ Ⓦ

Daylight lasts longer in the summer than the winter, and the Sun is higher in the sky. The changes follow a pattern that lasts 365.25 days. The model in diagram D explains this by saying that the Earth moves around the Sun.

The path it takes is called its **orbit**. The orbit is shaped like an **ellipse**. The length of time it takes a planet to travel once around the Sun is called a **year**.

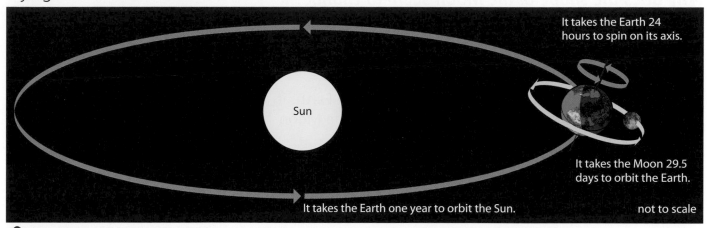

It takes the Earth 24 hours to spin on its axis.

Sun

It takes the Moon 29.5 days to orbit the Earth.

It takes the Earth one year to orbit the Sun.

not to scale

D *This is the model that astronomers use to explain years and the way the Moon appears.*

An Earth year is 365.25 days long. Our calendar has 365 days in every year, so every four years there is an extra day to make up the extra time. This day is added to the end of February in a **leap year**.

The Moon

The **Moon** appears to move across the sky once every 24 hours. It also seems to change shape. The changes of shape follow a pattern that lasts about 29.5 days. The model in diagram D explains this by saying that the Moon orbits (goes around) the Earth once every 29.5 days. This is called a **lunar month**.

E *The Moon can sometimes be seen during the day.*

A **satellite** is something that goes around a planet. The Moon is a **natural satellite** of the Earth.

4 a What is a year?
  b How long is an Earth year?
  c What is a leap year?

5 Which part of the model in diagram D explains: **H S W**
  a why we have day and night
  b why it takes 365 days between one midsummer and the next?

6 What is a satellite?

7 What is a lunar month?

8 Which part of the model in diagram D explains: **H S W**
  a the Moon appearing to travel across the sky once every 24 hours
  b the shape of the Moon appearing to change over 29.5 days?

I CAN...

o recall the lengths of days, months and years.
o describe a model which explains why we have days, nights and years. **H S W**
o describe what a satellite is.

Why does the shape of the Moon seem to change?

The Moon is the Earth's only natural satellite. It has no atmosphere. This means that there is no air, no wind and no rain. There is no life on the Moon.

The Moon is much smaller than the Earth. Like the Earth, it does not produce its own light. We can only see the Moon because it reflects sunlight back towards the Earth.

A *This is a footprint left by one of the Apollo astronauts. It will never be blown away.*

1 How big is the Moon compared with the Earth?
2 How are we able to see the Moon? Draw a diagram to explain your answer. (*Hint*: you may need to look back at the model on page 165.) Ⓗ Ⓢ Ⓦ
3 How do you think scientists know what it is like on the Moon? Ⓗ Ⓢ Ⓦ

The shape of the Moon seems to change as it orbits the Earth. The different shapes are called **phases of the Moon**. Half of the Moon is always lit by the Sun, but we cannot always see all of the lit part.

Sun • Moon • Earth • not to scale • From the Earth the Moon looks like this.

Sun • Moon • Earth • **B** not to scale • From the Earth the Moon looks like this.

Ⓗ Ⓢ Ⓦ
Thomas Hariot (1560–1621) observed the Moon using a telescope in 1609. He made the first detailed drawings of the Moon.

When the Moon is between the Sun and the Earth we cannot see any of the lit part. This is called the **new moon**. When we can see all of the lit part, the Moon looks like a complete circle. This is called a **full moon**. It takes 29.5 days for the Moon to orbit the Earth once. It is 29.5 days, or one lunar month, between one full moon and the next.

Eclipses

Sometimes the Moon is directly between the Sun and the Earth. Some places on the Earth are in the shadow of the Moon. People standing in the shadow see a **solar eclipse**. If the Sun is completely blocked out, we see a **total eclipse**. If only part of the Sun is blocked out, we see a **partial eclipse**.

Sometimes the Moon moves into the shadow of the Earth. When this happens the Moon looks very dark. This is a **lunar eclipse**. We do not get an eclipse every month because the orbit of the Moon is tilted compared to the orbit of the Earth.

4 How many days are there between one full moon and the next?

5 a Where is the Moon when there is a new moon?
  b Is a full moon visible during the day or at night? Explain your answer.

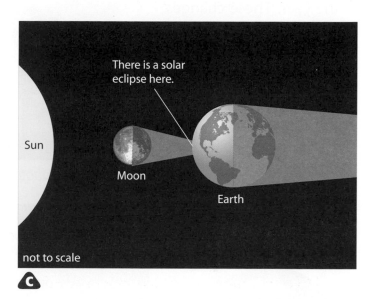

There is a solar eclipse here.

Sun

Moon

Earth

not to scale

C

6 Would a solar eclipse happen at full moon or new moon? Explain your answer.

7 Draw a diagram to show the positions of the Earth, the Moon and the Sun when there is a lunar eclipse. Show the rays from the Sun and where the shadow is. **H S W**

D The last total eclipse visible in the UK happened on 11 August 1999. During an eclipse scientists can study the Sun's atmosphere, which cannot normally be seen because it is not as bright as the Sun.

I CAN...

o explain how we can see the Moon.
o explain why the shape of the Moon seems to change as it moves around the Earth.
o use a model to show the arrangement of the Sun, Earth and Moon during a solar eclipse and a lunar eclipse. **H S W**

Why are summer and winter different?

The weather in Europe is very different at different times of the year. These changes happen because the Earth's axis is tilted.

1 Describe the differences between summer and winter for:
  a the length of daylight
  b the temperature.

A *These photos show the same place in summer and winter.*

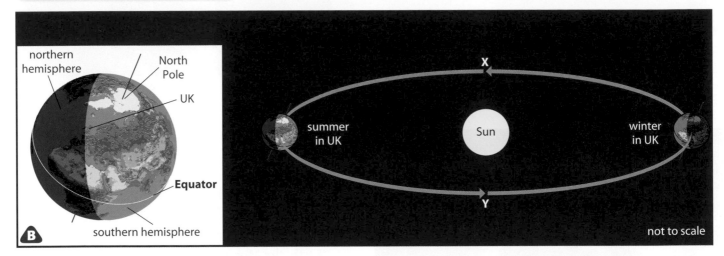

B

The Earth has two halves or **hemispheres**. Europe is in the northern hemisphere. When the **northern hemisphere** is tilted towards the Sun it is summer in Europe. The Sun is high in the sky at midday, and days are longer than nights.

When the northern hemisphere is tilted away from the Sun it is winter in Europe. The Sun is not very high in the sky at midday, and nights are longer than days.

2 Explain what a hemisphere is.
3 Look at diagram B.
  a What season will it be in the UK when the Earth is at position X?
  b What season will it be in the UK when the Earth is at position Y?
  c Explain your answers.

Ⓗ Ⓢ Ⓦ

In Roman times, the calendar was getting out of step with the seasons. Julius Caesar introduced a new calendar with 365 days in each year, and an extra day every fourth year (a leap year). The calendar got out of step again, and in 1582 Pope Gregory XIII amended it to remove some of the leap years. The Gregorian calendar was introduced in England in 1752, when 2 September was followed by 14 September.

4 Photo C shows the Earth from above the North Pole in July. Explain why days are longer than nights in summer. Ⓗ Ⓢ Ⓦ

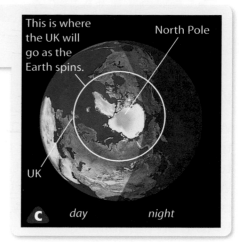

This is where the UK will go as the Earth spins.

North Pole

UK

C   day   night

The Sun feels hotter in the summer than it does in the winter. Some people think that this is because the Earth is closer to the Sun in summer, but this is not true in the northern hemisphere. The northern hemisphere is slightly closer to the Sun in winter. This means that the southern hemisphere is closer to the Sun during its summer, which is one reason why summers are often a little hotter in the southern hemisphere than they are in the northern hemisphere.

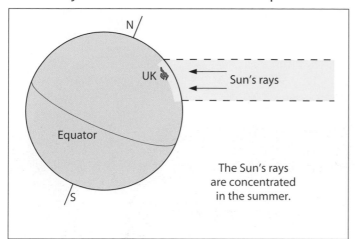

N

UK 👈   ← Sun's rays

Equator

S

The Sun's rays are concentrated in the summer.

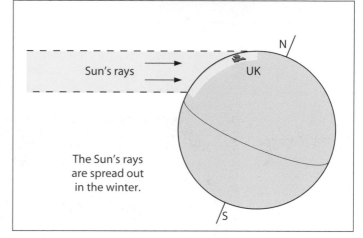

Sun's rays →   N

UK

S

The Sun's rays are spread out in the winter.

D

The Sun feels hotter in our summer because it is higher in the sky. This means the heat from the Sun is more concentrated. Summer days are also warmer than winter days because the Sun is shining for longer, and has more time to warm up the air and the ground.

5 Draw a diagram looking at the Earth from above the North Pole in winter (similar to photo C). Label your diagram to help you to explain why nights are longer than days in winter. Ⓗ Ⓢ Ⓦ

6 Australia is on the opposite side of the Earth to the UK. Which season is it in Australia when it is summer in the UK?

7 a If you were near the North Pole, how long would daylight last in summer? Ⓗ Ⓢ Ⓦ

  b What would happen in winter? Ⓗ Ⓢ Ⓦ

  c Draw labelled diagrams to explain your answers to parts **a** and **b**. Ⓗ Ⓢ Ⓦ

8 If you live near the Equator, the Sun always feels hotter than it does in the UK. Use a diagram to help you to explain why. Ⓗ Ⓢ Ⓦ

I CAN...

- list the differences between summer and winter in Europe.
- use a model to explain that we have seasons because the Earth's axis is tilted. Ⓗ Ⓢ ⓦ
- recall that the northern hemisphere is tilted towards the Sun in the summer.

What is the Solar System?

When people first started to observe the stars, they saw some points of light that appeared to move compared to the rest of the stars. We now know that these moving objects are planets orbiting the Sun. They are much closer to us than the stars.

There are eight planets in the **Solar System**, and three **dwarf planets** (Ceres, Pluto and Eris). There are also thousands of **asteroids** (small lumps of rock) and **comets** (mostly balls of dirty ice). Most of the planets have natural satellites (**moons**) orbiting them.

Asteroid belt

Sun

Ceres

Mars

Venus

Earth

Mercury

Jupiter

The planets are drawn to approximately the same scale.
The distances between them are not to scale.

A

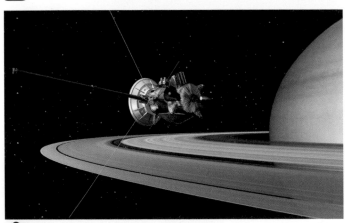

B *Scientists can observe other planets using telescopes on Earth. However, they can find out much more from the information sent back by space probes. This is an artist's impression of the Cassini probe orbiting Saturn.*

The four planets closest to the Sun are known as the **inner planets**. They are rocky planets. The other planets are the **outer planets**. The outer planets are made of gas. The further a planet is from the Sun, the longer it takes to orbit it.

1 Write down the names of the inner planets, starting with the one closest to the Sun.

2 Which planets are made of gas?

3 Which planet has the longest year? Explain your answer.

Most of the asteroids have orbits between Mars and Jupiter, but some have orbits which cross the orbit of the Earth. Many scientists think that the dinosaurs were wiped out when an asteroid hit the Earth 65 million years ago.

You can sometimes see planets in the night sky. We can see planets because they reflect light from the Sun. They do not make their own light. Planets look brighter than stars because they are much closer to the Earth.

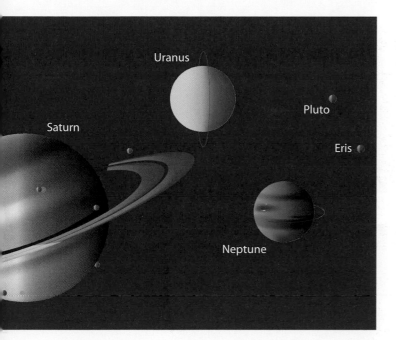

The Earth is the only planet that has living things on it. The other planets are too hot or too cold.

6 a Draw a bar chart showing the mean temperature of each planet. Ⓗ Ⓢ Ⓦ
  b Describe the pattern you can see from your graph. Ⓗ Ⓢ Ⓦ
  c The asteroids are about 400 million km from the Sun. Use your graph to estimate the mean temperature on an asteroid. Ⓗ Ⓢ Ⓦ
  d One planet does not fit the pattern on the graph. Find out why this planet does not follow the pattern. Ⓗ Ⓢ Ⓦ

4 a What is an asteroid?
  b Between which two planets are the orbits of most of the asteroids?
5 How can we see planets in the night sky?

Planet	Distance from Sun (million km)	Mean surface temperature (°C)
Mercury	58	170
Venus	108	460
Earth	150	15
Mars	228	−50
Jupiter	778	−143
Saturn	1427	−195
Uranus	2870	−201
Neptune	4497	−220

Ⓒ

Ⓗ Ⓢ Ⓦ

A Polish astronomer called Copernicus (1473–1543) suggested that the planets went around the Sun. Until that time most people thought that everything went around the Earth. In 1610, another astronomer called Galileo (1564–1642) proved that Copernicus was correct by using one of the first telescopes. The Christian church believed that the Earth was at the centre of the Solar System, and Galileo was arrested when he wrote about his theory.

I CAN...

o describe how planets, dwarf planets and asteroids are arranged in the Solar System.
o explain why planets look brighter than stars.

Could there ever have been life on Mars?

People have been able to see Mars for thousands of years, but it was not until the invention of the telescope that astronomers could look for features on its surface.

Giovanni Schiaparelli (1835–1910) published a map of Mars in 1877 and regularly updated it with new observations. He drew some straight features, which he called channels.

Schiaparelli's map got a lot of people interested. Perhaps the channels were artificial? This would mean there could be intelligent life on Mars. People could see the polar ice caps on Mars, which meant there was some water there, and water is essential for life to exist. The dark and light areas also looked like land and oceans. If there was water on the planet, it was possible that life existed on Mars.

Percival Lowell (1855–1916) was keen on this idea. He carried out observations of his own, and published books supporting the idea of life on Mars.

Other scientists thought that there was no liquid water on Mars, as the atmosphere was too thin. The answer came in 1964, when Mariner 4 flew past Mars. It sent pictures back to Earth which showed rocky land with no water and no plants.

> **!**
> The biggest volcano in the Solar System is Olympus Mons on Mars. It is 25 km high.

HowScienceWorks

A *An updated map published by Schiaparellli in 1888.*

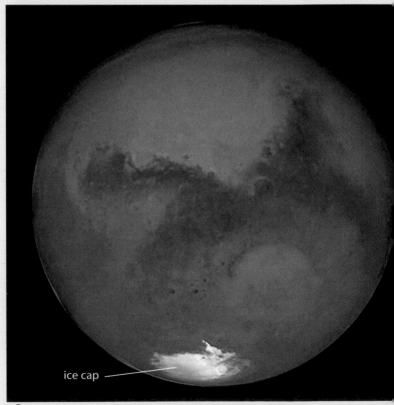

ice cap

B *This photograph of Mars was taken by the Hubble Space Telescope.*

Mars exploration highlights

Over half of the spacecraft sent to investigate Mars never got there, or crashed on landing. These are some of the successful ones.

1964 First flypast of the planet by Mariner 4.

1971 Mars 2, sent by the former USSR, was the first spacecraft to go into orbit around Mars. It orbited for nearly a year and sent back information about the surface and the atmosphere. The lander it sent down crashed.

1976 The Viking 1 lander was the first spacecraft to land safely on Mars. It carried out some experiments on the Martian soil. Most scientists agree that the experiments did not detect any signs that life existed there.

1997 Mars Global Surveyor went into orbit around Mars. It sent back detailed pictures and photos for nearly 10 years. Some ground features in the images are similar to features on Earth that were formed by flowing water.

2003 Mars Express went into orbit around Mars. This was the first spacecraft sent to another planet by the European Space Agency. It is sending back very detailed images and information about the types of rock on the surface. The lander it sent down (Beagle 2) crashed.

2004 Two NASA rovers, Spirit and Opportunity, landed on Mars.

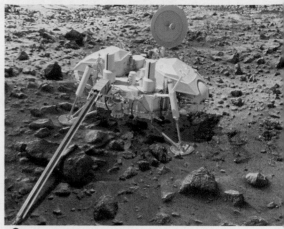

C *An artist's impression of Viking 1 on Mars.*

D *Artist's impression of Spirit on Mars.*

E *The surface of Mars, made up from photographs taken by the Spirit rover.*

1 Why do scientists want to find out if there is water on Mars?

2 a Before 1964, some people thought there might be life on Mars. Describe the evidence for and against this idea.

b What new evidence has been found since 1964?

3 How has technology helped scientists to find out more about Mars?

4 Most of the spacecraft sent to investigate other planets have gone to Mars. Suggest as many reasons for this as you can.

What is beyond the Solar System?

When you look at the sky on a clear night you can see lots of **stars**. Stars are huge balls of gas that give out large amounts of light and heat. The Sun is a star. The stars you see at night do not seem very bright compared to the Sun because they are much further away. The stars are around us all the time. We cannot see them during the day because the light they give out is very faint compared with the light from the Sun.

A

> 1 What is a star?
> 2 Why does the Sun look much brighter than the other stars?
> 3 Why can't we see stars during the day?

If you look carefully at the stars you can see patterns, called **constellations**. Long ago people thought that gods lived in the sky, and named some of the patterns after gods or animals. People in different cultures found different patterns in the stars. The names we use today are the ones that were used in Europe.

The stars in a constellation are not really close together. They only look close when we look at them from the Earth.

> 4 What is a constellation?
> 5 If astronomers watch the stars all night, they have to keep moving their telescopes as the stars seem to move across the sky. Why does this happen? (*Hint*: you may need to look back at Topic 7La.) Ⓗ Ⓢ Ⓦ

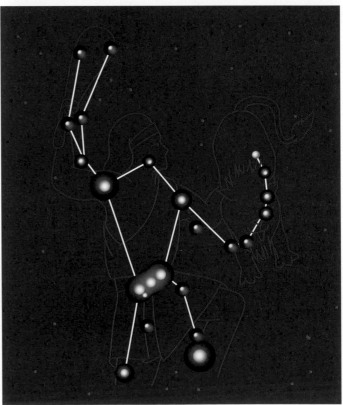

Ⓑ *This is the constellation Orion.*

C *This time-lapse photograph shows how the stars appear to move during the night.*

Galaxies

When people first observed the stars they saw fuzzy patches of light. When telescopes were invented, people could see these patches of light more clearly. Some of them were large groups of stars, called **galaxies**.

The Sun is in a galaxy called the **Milky Way**. The bright band of stars in photo A is part of the Milky Way. It is the part of our galaxy that we can see from Earth. There are millions of other galaxies, and each of these galaxies contains millions of stars. All these galaxies make up the **Universe**.

H S W

In 1784, Charles Messier (1730–1817) published the final part of his list of fuzzy objects in the sky. There were just over 100 objects in it. We now know that many of these objects are galaxies.

7 If astronomers look at a galaxy, what would they be looking at?

8 Astronomers think that there are at least 100 billion galaxies in the Universe. Why did Messier only list 100 of them? H S W

The stars are a very long way apart. Scientists measure these distances in **light years**. One light year is the distance travelled by light in one year. It works out as 10 000 000 000 000 000 km (ten thousand million million km).

The nearest star to the Sun is called Proxima Centauri. It is 4.22 light years away. It would take a rocket from Earth over 12 000 years to reach Proxima Centauri.

6 Does a 'light year' measure distance or time? H S W

D *This is the Andromeda galaxy. It is the nearest large galaxy to the Milky Way. Scientists think that our galaxy looks something like this.*

I CAN...

- describe what a star is and explain why we can only see them at night.
- use a model to explain why the stars appear to move across the sky. H S W
- explain what the words constellation, galaxy, Milky Way and Universe mean.

HowScienceworks

Should we be spending money on studying the Universe?

A *This photograph was taken by the Hubble Space Telescope. It shows the remains of an exploded star.*

The Hubble Space Telescope orbits the Earth. It takes very detailed photographs of distant stars and galaxies. It is estimated that the total cost of building it and running it will be around $6 billion (about £3 000 000 000) by the time it stops working.

B Sailors used to use stars to navigate their ships. This is a sextant. It can be pointed at certain stars to find the position of a ship.

C The European Space Agency spends about £2 000 000 000 a year. The money comes from the taxpayers in different European countries. That's enough to build seven or eight new hospitals every year!

D We know so much more about the Universe than people did 100 years ago, but there is so much more to find out!

E People used to need to know about the stars for navigation, but we can do that in other ways now. Why spend more money? It won't help anyone here on Earth.

HAVE YOUR SAY

Do you think that money should be spent on finding out more about the planets and the stars?

1 a How did people study the stars and planets 200 years ago?
   b What technology do we have now that allows us to study the stars and planets?
2 Write down some facts about the Solar System or the stars that have been discovered using technology.
3 Why do you think that astronomers still study the planets and stars?

Glossary

Pronunciation note: A capital 'O' is said as in 'so'

abdomen	Rear or bottom end of an animal's main body.
abrade	To wear down by knocking into things.
abrasion	When rock fragments bump into each other and wear away.
acetic acid (*a-see-tick*)	The old name for ethanoic acid. It is the acid in vinegar.
acid	A substance that turns litmus red. It has a pH of less than 7.
acid rain	Rain containing sulphuric and nitric acids.
acne (*ack-nee*)	Spots on the skin.
adaptations (*add-app-tay-shuns*)	The features that plants and animals have to help them live in a particular place.
adapted	When something has certain features to do a particular function.
adolescence (*add-ol-less-sense*)	Time when both physical and emotional changes occur in teenagers.
afterbirth	When the placenta is pushed out through the vagina.
aggregate	Sand, gravel and other stones used in building roads and making concrete.
air pressure (*air presh-ur*)	The pressure of the air around us.
air resistance	A force that tries to slow things that are moving through air down. It is a type of friction.
alkali (*alk-al-lie*)	Substance that turns litmus blue. It has a pH of more than 7.
ammeter	A piece of equipment that measures how much electricity is flowing around a circuit.
amnion (*am-nee-on*)	Bag containing amniotic fluid.
amniotic fluid (*am-nee-ot-tick*)	Liquid surrounding the growing embryo and protecting it.
amp (A)	The unit for measuring current.
amphibian (*am-fib-ee-an*)	Vertebrate with moist skin (e.g. a frog).
antacid (*ant-ass-id*)	A medicine containing an alkali used to neutralise some of the acid in the stomach to treat heartburn.
ante-natal class	Many pregnant women attend these classes to find out more about pregnancy and childbirth. They learn ways to cope with any problems.
antenna	Something sticking out of an animal's head which is used to sense things. Plural: antennae.
antibodies	Substances produced by white blood cells that help to fight microbes that might cause diseases.
arachnid (*ar-ack-nid*)	Type of arthropod with four pairs of legs (e.g. a spider).
arthropod (*arth-row-pod*)	Invertebrate with jointed legs (e.g. a fly or spider).
ascorbic acid (*a-score-bick*)	Chemical name for vitamin C.
asteroid (*ass-ter-oyd*)	A small lump of rock orbiting the Sun.
astronomer	A scientist who studies the planets, stars and other things in space.
astronomy	The study of the Universe, including all the stars and planets.
atom	The smallest part of an element.
axis (*acks-iss*)	Imaginary vertical line that goes from one pole of the Earth to the other. The Earth spins around its axis.
balanced forces	Two forces that are the same strength and working in opposite directions.
battery	Two or more cells used together.
behaviour	The way an organism acts or reacts to things around it.

biodiesel (*bi-O-dee-zel*)	A fuel made from vegetable oils that can be used in car engines that were originally designed to use diesel fuel.
biofuel	A fuel made from plants or from animal droppings.
biological weathering	When rocks are worn away or broken up due to the activities of living things. For example, growing plant roots can split rocks apart.
biomass fuel (*bi-O-mass*)	A fuel that comes from plants, animals, or their wastes (e.g. wood, methane from rotting plants).
biopsy	Taking a small sample of tissue to test for diseases and other problems.
bird	Vertebrate with feathers (e.g. an eagle).
bonds	Forces holding particles together.
brain	Organ that controls what the body does.
braking distance	The distance a car travels while the brakes are trying to stop it.
breathing system (*bree-thing*)	Organ system that takes in oxygen and gets rid of carbon dioxide from our bodies.
bulb	Plant organ that is usually underground. Some plants only have leaves at certain times of the year and remain as bulbs at other times.
cable	The wire for something that runs off mains electricity. It has three separate wires inside it.
cable grip	Part of a plug that holds the cable, and stops the wires being pulled out of the pins.
calcium carbonate	The chemical from which the shells of most sea creatures are made. The main chemical in rocks such as limestone and chalk.
carbon dioxide	A gas which will put out a lighted splint and turn limewater milky. Produced when acids react with limestone.
carnivore	An animal that only eats other animals.
cell (*sell*) (biology)	The basic unit which living things are made from.
cell (physics)	A source of electricity with a low 'energy' (low voltage). Cells push electrons round a circuit.
cell division	When a cell splits in two. Cells are made using cell division.
cell surface membrane (*mem-brayn*)	Controls what goes into and out of a cell.
cell wall	Tough wall around plant cells. Helps to support the cell.
cellulose (*sell-U-lOse*)	Tough material that plant cell walls are made from.
cementation (*sem-men-tay-shun*)	A process in which water is squeezed out of the spaces between pieces of rock leaving mineral salts behind which stick (cement) the rock pieces together.
cement (*sem-men*)	To stick something together.
centipede (*sent-ip-eed*)	Type of arthropod with a long thin body divided into sections. One pair of legs on each body section.
cervix (*sir-vicks*)	Ring of muscle at the bottom of the uterus in females.
chalk	Soft white or grey rock formed from the shells of small sea animals.
chemical energy	The kind of energy stored in chemicals. Food, fuel and batteries all contain chemical energy.
chemical reaction	A reaction in which new substances are made.
chemical weathering	When rocks are broken up or worn away by chemical reactions, usually with rainwater.
chlorophyll (*klor-O-fill*)	Green substance found inside chloroplasts.
chloroplast (*klor-O-plast*)	Green disc containing chlorophyll. Found in plant cells. Where the plant makes food using photosynthesis.

choice chamber	Equipment that allows scientists to test how environmental factors affect organisms.
cilia (sil-lee-ah)	Small hairs on the surface of some cells.
ciliated epithelial cell (sil-lee-ay-ted ep-pee-theel-ee-al)	Cell with cilia found in the lungs.
circuit (sir-kit)	A complete loop that electricity flows around.
circulatory system (serk-you-late-or-ee)	Organ system that carries oxygen and food around the body.
circumcision (sir-cum-siz-shun)	Removal of the foreskin.
citric acid (sit-rick)	The acid in citrus fruits.
classification (clas-if-ik-ay-shun)	Sorting things into groups.
cloning (clO-ning)	A way of making new organisms from part of one organism (both males and females are not needed).
coal	A fossil fuel made from the remains of plants.
coarse focusing wheel	Wheel on a microscope that moves parts of the microscope a large amount to get the image into focus.
combustion	The scientific word for burning.
comet	A small lump of dirty ice orbiting the Sun.
community (com-mew-nit-ee)	All the plants and animals that live in a habitat.
compaction (com-pack-shun)	When layers of sediment or rock are squashed by the weight of sediment above them.
compete	When two or more organisms struggle against one another to get the same things (e.g. food).
competition	Some organisms need the same things as each other. We say that they compete for those things.
component (com-po-nent)	Something in a circuit, like a bulb, switch or motor.
concentrated	Something that has a large amount of the substance in it (and very little water or other impurities).
conclusion	What the results of an investigation show.
constellation (con-stell-ay-shun)	A pattern of stars.
consumer (con-syou-mer)	An organism that has to eat other organisms to stay alive. Animals are consumers.
contact force	A force that needs to touch an object before it can affect it (e.g. friction).
continuous variation	Data values that change gradually (e.g. time, lengths).
contract	Get smaller.
contractions (con-track-shuns)	The uterus muscles squeezing.
convection current (con-veck-shun)	A flow of liquid or gas caused by part of it being heated or cooled more than the rest.
cord	See 'umbilical cord'.
correlation	Same as a relationship.
corrosion	When stone or metal reacts with chemicals in air or water and is worn away or changed into a different substance.
corrosive (cor-row-sive)	Substances that attack metals, stonework and skin are called corrosive.
coverslip	Thin piece of glass used to hold a specimen in place on a slide.
crustacean (crust-ay-shun)	Type of arthropod with a chalky shell and 5–7 pairs of legs (e.g. a lobster).
crystals (kris-tals)	Pieces of a mineral with sharp edges.
cubic centimetre (cm³)	A unit used for measuring volumes.
cytoplasm (site-O-plaz-m)	Jelly inside a cell where the cell's activities happen.
daily changes	Changes in the physical environmental factors which happen during a day (e.g. it gets dark at night).
data	Information collected in experiments.

daughter cell	The two new cells made by cell division.
day	The time it takes for a planet to spin once on its axis. This takes 24 hours on Earth.
deciduous tree (dess-idd-you-us)	Tree that drops its leaves in winter (e.g. oak tree).
decomposer	Something that eats dead plants.
decompose	When one substance splits up into two or more products.
dense	Something that is heavy for its volume.
density	The amount of mass that 1 cm³ of a substance has. Measured in g/cm³.
deposit	When moving water drops rock fragments or grains.
detonator	Something that will start a reaction (often used with explosives or fireworks).
dialysis machine (dye-al-ee-sis)	Machine that removes waste from the blood in people whose kidneys are not working properly.
diffusion (diff-you-zshun)	When particles spread and mix with each other without anything moving them.
digestive system (die-jest-iv)	Organ system that breaks down our food.
dilute (die-lyoot)	Make something less concentrated.
discontinuous variation	Data values that do not have a continuous range of options (e.g. days of the week, shoe sizes).
displace	To push out of the way.
distance–time graph	A graph that shows how far and how fast something travels during a journey.
distribution (diss-trib-you-shun)	The places where an organism can be found in a habitat.
dwarf planet	A rocky body orbiting the Sun that is not quite big enough to be called a planet (e.g. Pluto).
Earth	The planet we live on.
earth wire	The green and yellow wire in a cable or plug. It is there for safety.
echinoderm (ek-eye-no-derm)	Invertebrate with a body in five parts (e.g. a starfish).
ecologist (eck-oll-O-jist)	Scientist who studies organisms and the areas where they live.
egg cell	The female sex cell.
ejaculation (edge-ack-you-lay-shun)	Semen is pumped out of a man's penis into the top of the vagina during sexual intercourse.
elastic	Any substance that will return to its original shape and size after it has been stretched or squashed.
electric current	The flow of electricity around a circuit.
electric shock	The effect of electricity flowing through the body.
electrical conductor	A material that lets electricity flow through it.
electrical insulator	A material that does not let electricity flow through it.
electricity	A way of transferring energy through wires.
electron	Tiny particle that flows around a circuit.
ellipse	A shape like a squashed circle.
embryo (em-bree-O)	Tiny new human life which grows by cell division from a fertilised egg cell.
endangered (en-dayn-jerd)	When a type of organism is in danger of ceasing to exist.
energy resources	Stores of energy that we need for heating, transport and to keep our bodies working.
environment	The conditions around a certain organism caused by physical environmental factors.
environmental factors	Things in an environment that can change something about an organism.
environmental variation	Differences between organisms caused by environmental factors.
Equator (ee-kwate-er)	An imaginary line around the middle of the Earth.
erection	When the penis becomes stiff.
erosion (eh-rO-shun)	The movement of loose and weathered rock.
estimate	To work out an approximate answer to something using rough figures.

ethanoic acid (*eth-an-nO-ic*)	The acid in vinegar.
evergreen tree	Tree that keeps its leaves in winter (e.g. pine tree).
evidence	Observations, data or measurements that scientists will use to test whether their ideas are correct or not.
excrete (*ex-kreet*)	Get rid of waste materials from an organism.
excretory system (*ex-kree-torr-ee*)	Organ system that removes poisonous substances from your body. It includes the kidneys, liver and bladder.
exoskeleton (*ex-O-skel-e-ton*)	Thick outer covering found on arthropods.
expand	Get bigger.
explosive	A chemical that reacts very fast, giving out a lot of energy and making lots of gas.
external development	When offspring develop outside a mother.
external fertilisation	When fertilisation happens outside the bodies of the parents.
eyepiece lens	Part of the microscope you look down.
feeding relationship	How organisms in a habitat rely on each other for food.
fertilisation (*fert-ill-eyes-ay-shun*)	Fusing of a male sex cell with a female sex cell.
fertilised egg cell	What is produced when a sperm cell fuses with an egg cell.
filament	Thin piece of wire inside a light bulb that glows when electricity is flowing through it.
fine focusing wheel	Wheel on a microscope that moves parts of the microscope a small amount to focus the image.
fire extinguisher (*ex-ting-wish-er*)	Something that puts out a fire.
fire triangle	A way of showing in a diagram that heat, oxygen and fuel are needed for a fire.
fish	Vertebrate with wet scales, fins and gills (e.g. a salmon).
flow	Move and change shape smoothly.
flower	Organ used for reproduction in plants.
focus	Make an image clear and sharp.
foetus (*fee-tus*)	After an embryo has grown all its organs it is called a foetus. This is usually after about 10 weeks.
food chain	A way of showing what eats what in a habitat.
food web	Many food chains linked together.
foodpipe	Another term for 'gullet'.
force	A push or a pull.
force meter	Piece of equipment containing a spring, used to measure forces.
foreskin	A covering of skin protecting the head of the penis.
fossil	The remains of a dead animal or plant that became trapped in layers of sediment and turned into rock.
fossil fuels	Coal, oil and natural gas – all fuels that were formed from the remains of dead plants and animals.
free range	Farm animals that are allowed to roam around outside and have plenty of space.
freeze–thaw action	A type of physical weathering that happens when water gets into a crack in a rock and freezes. The freezing water expands and makes the crack bigger.
friction	A force that slows things down when two things rub against each other.
fuel	Anything that stores energy that can be converted into heat energy, e.g. fossil fuels and nuclear fuel.
fuel cell	A machine that combines hydrogen and oxygen gases to produce electricity.
full moon	The phase of the Moon when it looks like a bright, full circle.
function	Something's job.
fuse (biology)	When two sex cells join together to form a fertilised egg cell they are said to fuse.
fuse (physics)	A piece of wire that melts if too much electricity flows through it.

galaxy	Millions of stars grouped together.
gas	Something that does not have a fixed shape or volume, and is easy to squash.
generate	Produce electricity by turning a magnet inside coils of wire.
geologist	A scientist who studies rocks.
geothermal power (*gee-O-therm-al*)	Making electricity using heat from rocks underground.
gestation period (*jess-tay-shun*)	The length of time from fertilisation to birth.
glacier	Ice that fills a valley and moves slowly downhill.
glands	The glands in the male reproductive system add a special liquid to the sperm cells to make semen. There are other sorts of glands in the body.
global warming	A theory that says that the Earth is getting hotter because of the activities of humans. It may be caused by too much carbon dioxide in the air.
grafts	When part of one plant is fixed to another plant.
grain	Tiny piece of a rock or mineral.
gram (g)	A unit for measuring mass.
gravity	The force of attraction between any two objects. The Earth is very big and so has strong gravity that pulls everything down towards it.
gullet (*gull-ett*)	Organ in the shape of a tube that takes food from your mouth to your stomach.
habitat	The place an organism lives in (e.g. woodland).
harmful	Something that causes harm, but less dangerous than a corrosive substance.
hazard	Something that could be a danger.
head	Front or top end of an animal's body.
heart	Organ that pumps blood.
heart transplant	When the heart from someone who has died is used to replace a damaged heart in someone else.
hemispheres (*hem-ee-sfears*)	The two halves of a sphere – the shape you would get if you cut a solid ball in half.
herbivore	An animal that only eats plants.
hibernation (*high-ber-nay-shun*)	When animals hide during the winter and go to sleep.
host	The organism that a parasite lives in or on.
hydrocarbon	A chemical compound containing only hydrogen and carbon.
hydrochloric acid (*hy-drO-klor-ick*)	A common acid that is found in your stomach.
hydroelectric power (*hy-drO-el-eck-trick*)	Making electricity by letting falling water (usually from a reservoir) turn turbines and generators.
igneous rock	A rock formed from interlocking crystals.
image	What you see down a microscope.
implantation (*im-plant-ay-shun*)	When an embryo sinks into the soft lining of the uterus.
impulse	Electrical signal carried by a nerve cell.
indicator (*ind-ic-ay-ter*)	A dye that will change colour in acids and alkalis.
inherit	Getting a characteristic from a parent.
inherited variation	Differences between organisms passed to offspring by their parents in reproduction.
inner planets	Mercury, Venus, Earth and Mars. The inner planets are all rocky planets.
insect	Type of arthropod with three pairs of legs (e.g. a fly).
interlocking	When crystals fit with no gaps between them.
internal development	When offspring animals develop inside a mother.
internal fertilisation	When fertilisation happens inside the body of a parent.
invertebrate (*in-vert-eb-rate*)	Animal with no backbone.
irreversible	Permanent change which can't be reversed.
irritant	Something that irritates the skin and eyes.

IVF (in vitro fertilisation)	Fertilisation happens outside the woman in a dish. The embryo develops and is then placed inside her.
joule (J) (jool)	The unit for measuring energy.
kidneys	Organs used to clean the blood and make urine.
kilogram (kg)	A unit for measuring mass. There are 1000 g in 1 kg.
kilojoule (kJ) (kill-O-jool)	There are 1000 joules in 1 kilojoule.
kilometres per hour (km/h)	Units for speed when the distance is measured in kilometres and the time is measured in hours.
kingdom	Largest group that living things are sorted into. The two biggest are the plant and animal kingdoms.
labour	Time when the baby is about to be born.
landfill site	Large area in which rubbish is left.
large intestine (in-test-in)	Organ that removes water from unwanted food.
law of conservation of energy	The idea that energy can never be created or destroyed, only changed from one form into another.
leaf	Plant organ used to make food by photosynthesis.
leap year	A year with 366 days in it. We have a leap year every 4 years.
lifecycle	The series of changes in an organism as it gets older.
light year	The distance that light travels in one year.
limestone	A sedimentary rock made from the shells of dead sea creatures consisting mainly of calcium carbonate.
limewater	A chemical that goes cloudy when carbon dioxide is bubbled through it.
liquid (lick-wid)	Something with a fixed volume but no fixed shape.
litmus	A simple kind of indicator. It turns red in acids and blue in alkalis.
live wire	The brown wire in a cable or plug.
liver	Organ used to make and destroy substances.
lubricant (loo-brick-ant)	A substance (normally a liquid) used to reduce friction.
lubrication (loo-brick-ay-shun)	Adding a lubricant to something.
lunar eclipse	When the Moon moves into the shadow of the Earth.
lunar month	29.5 days – the time it takes the Moon to orbit the Earth once.
lungs	Organs used to take oxygen out of the air and put waste carbon dioxide into the air.
magnetism	A force that attracts objects made out of iron.
magnification (mag-nif-ick-ay-shun)	How much bigger a microscope makes something appear.
magnify (mag-nif-eye)	To make something look bigger.
mains electricity	Electricity provided to houses, shops, etc. from power stations.
mammal	Vertebrate with hair, which also produces milk (e.g. a human).
mammary glands	Glands contained in the breasts of women, which produce milk after childbirth.
mass	The amount of matter that something is made of. Mass is measured in grams (g) and kilograms (kg). Your mass does not change if you go into space or to another planet.
mature	Another word for develop.
menopause (men-O-paws)	When the ovaries in women stop releasing eggs.
menstrual cycle (men-strew-al)	Series of events lasting about a month, happening in the female reproductive system. The cycle causes ovulation and the lining of the uterus is replaced.

menstruation (men-strew-ay-shun)	When the lining of the uterus and a little blood pass out of the vagina as part of the menstrual cycle.
metal	Substance that allows heat and electricity to pass through it.
metamorphic rock	A rock formed from interlocking crystals that are often lined up in layers.
metres per second (m/s)	Units for speed when the distance is measured in metres and the time is measured in seconds.
microhabitat	Small areas of a habitat with certain conditions (e.g. under a log in a woodland habitat).
microscope (my-crow-scope)	Used to magnify small things.
migration (my-gray-shun)	When animals move to different areas of the world depending on the season.
miles per hour (mph)	Units for speed when the distance is measured in miles and the time is measured in hours.
Milky Way	The galaxy that our Solar System is in.
millipede (mill-ip-eed)	Arthropod with long, thin body divided into sections. Two pairs of legs on each body section.
minerals	The chemicals that rocks are made from.
mixture	Two or more different kinds of mineral that are not chemically joined to each other.
model	A scientific way of thinking about how or why things happen.
mollusc (moll-usk)	Invertebrate that crawls on a fleshy pad (e.g. a snail).
moon	A natural satellite of a planet.
Moon	The Moon (with a capital M) is the moon that orbits the Earth.
muscle cell (muss-ell)	Cell that can change its length and so help us to move.
natural gas	Fossil fuel formed from the remains of dead plants and animals that lived in the sea.
natural satellite	Anything that orbits a planet that has not been made by humans.
navel (nave-ell)	Scar left by the umbilical cord. Often called the 'belly button'.
nerve	Groups of special cells that carry messages around the body. Nerves are made of many nerve cells.
nerve cell	Cell that carries signals around the body.
nervous system (nerve-us)	Organ system that carries signals around the body.
neuron (or neurone) (nyour-on) (nyour-own)	Another name for a nerve cell.
neutral	Substance that is neither an acid nor an alkali. It has a pH of 7.
neutral wire	The blue wire in a cable or plug.
neutralisation	When something is neutralised.
neutralise	When something is added to an acid or an alkali to make it more neutral – closer to pH7.
new moon	The phase of the Moon when we cannot see the lit-up side.
newton (N)	The unit of force.
newton meter	Another name for a force meter.
nitric acid (ny-trick)	A common acid.
nocturnal (nock-tur-nal)	Organisms that are active at night are nocturnal.
non-contact force	A force that can affect something from a distance (e.g. gravity).
non-renewable	Any energy resource that will run out and we cannot renew our supplies of it (e.g. oil).
normal distribution	When many things are a middle value with fewer things having greater or lesser values. This sort of data forms a bell shape on charts and graphs.
northern hemisphere	The half of the Earth with the North Pole in it. The UK is in the northern hemisphere.
nuclear power	Generating electricity by using the energy stored inside uranium.

nucleus (*new-clee-us*)	The 'control centre' of a cell. Plural: nuclei.
nutrition (*new-trish-on*)	Another word for food.
objective lens	Part of the microscope that is closest to what you are looking at.
observations	Information collected in experiments (e.g. what you see happening, measurements you make).
offspring	Any plant or animal formed by reproduction. Offspring are produced by their parents.
oil	Fossil fuel formed from the remains of dead plants and animals that lived in the sea.
omnivore	An animal that eats both plants and other animals.
onion-skin weathering	A type of physical weathering that happens when a rock is heated and cooled over and over again.
oolite (*oo-lite*)	A type of limestone formed when water evaporates and leaves calcium carbonate behind.
orbit	The path that a planet takes around a star, or the path that a moon or satellite takes around a planet.
organ	A large part of a plant or animal that has a very important function. It is made from different tissues.
organ system	Collection of organs working together to do a very important function.
organic	Something that has been produced without the use of lots of artificial chemicals.
organism	A living thing.
outer planets	Jupiter, Saturn, Uranus and Neptune. The outer planets are all mostly gas.
ovary (*O-very*)	Female reproductive organ. Produces egg cells.
oviduct	Carries egg cells from the ovaries to the uterus in women. Fertilisation happens here.
ovulation (*ov-you-lay-shun*)	Release of an egg cell from an ovary in women.
oxide	A compound that includes oxygen.
palisade cell (*pal-iss-aid*)	Cell found in leaves that contains many chloroplasts.
parallel circuit	A circuit with two or more branches that split apart and join up again.
parasite	Organism that lives in or on another living thing (its host) and gets its food from its host.
parent	An organism that has had offspring.
partial eclipse	A solar eclipse when the Moon only covers part of the Sun.
particles (*part-ick-als*)	The tiny pieces that everything is made out of.
particle theory	Theory that says that all materials are made out of particles that are constantly moving.
permanent	A change in which what you ended up with cannot be turned back into what you started with.
permeable	Permeable rocks let water soak through them.
pH scale	A numbered scale from 1 to 14 showing the strengths of acids and alkalis. Numbers below 7 are acids. Numbers above 7 are alkalis. pH 7 is neutral.
phases of the Moon	The different shapes the Moon seems to have at different times.
photosynthesis (*foto-sinth-e-sis*)	Process that plants use to make their own food. It needs light to work. Carbon dioxide and water are used up. Food (a sugar called glucose) and oxygen are produced.
physical change (*fizz-ick-al*)	A change that does not involve new chemicals being made. Melting and freezing are examples of physical changes.
physical environmental factors (*fizz-ick-cal*)	The non-living conditions in the environment of an organism (e.g. temperature, light).
physical weathering	When rocks are worn away or broken up by physical processes such as changes in temperature.
pickling	When foods are preserved by keeping them in vinegar.

placenta (*plas-en-ta*)	Attached to the uterus wall, this takes oxygen and food out of the mother's blood and puts waste materials into the mother's blood.
planet	A large object orbiting a star. The Earth is a planet.
pooter	A small container connected to two tubes. Used to catch tiny animals.
porous (*poor-us*)	Porous rocks have tiny holes in them.
power pack	A source of electricity with a low 'energy' (low voltage).
predator	An animal that catches and eats other animals.
prediction	What you think will happen in an experiment.
pregnant	When a woman has an embryo growing inside her uterus.
premature	A premature baby is small and born early.
pressure (*presh-ur*)	The force caused by particles hitting a certain area.
prey (*pray*)	An animal that is caught and eaten by another animal.
producer (*prod-you-sur*)	An organism that is able to make its own food. Plants are producers.
product	A new chemical formed in a chemical reaction.
property	A description of how a material behaves and what it is like. Hardness is a property of some solids.
puberty (*pew-bert-ty*)	Time when big physical changes happen in the body of a teenager.
quadrat (*kwad-rat*)	A square frame, thrown randomly on the ground, which is used to sample plants in an area.
radiation (*ray-dee-ay-shun*)	Dangerous particles and energy given off by uranium and other radioactive materials.
reactants	Chemicals that join together to form new substances.
relationship	A link between two things, so that when one thing changes so does the other. Best seen by using a graph.
renewable	An energy resource that will never run out (e.g. solar power).
reproductive organs	Organs used in sexual reproduction.
reproductive system	All the reproductive organs.
reptile	Vertebrate with dry scales (e.g. a snake).
resistance	A way of saying how difficult it is for electricity to flow through something.
resistor	A component that makes it difficult for electricity to flow – resistors are used to reduce the size of the current in a circuit.
reversible	A change in which what you end up with can easily be turned back into what you started with.
risk assessment	A way of estimating the amount of risk involved in an activity (and of taking steps to reduce the risk where necessary).
root	Plant organ used to take water out of the soil.
root hair cell	Cell found in roots. It has a large surface area to help the cell absorb water quickly.
root hair tissue	Found in roots. Takes in water from the soil.
rust	Substance formed when iron or steel reacts with oxygen and water.
sample	Taking a small part of something to investigate. A large sample size gives more reliable data.
satellite	Anything that orbits a planet.
scientific method	When scientists think up ideas to explain things and then test those ideas.
scrotum (*scrow-tum*)	Bag of skin containing the testes in males.
seasonal changes	Changes in the physical environmental factors of an environment which happen during the course of a year (e.g. it gets colder in winter).
sediment	Rock grains and fragments dropped on the bottom of a river, lake or sea.
sedimentary rock	A rock formed from grains stuck together. The grains are often rounded.

seed	A tiny part of a plant formed by sexual reproduction that can grow into a new plant.
semen (see-men)	A mixture of sperm cells and special fluids released by men during sexual intercourse.
series circuit	A circuit in which there is only one loop of wire.
sex cell	A cell used for sexual reproduction.
sex hormones (hor-moans)	Chemicals released in our bodies that control the menstrual cycle and puberty.
sexual reproduction	Producing new organisms by the joining of two sex cells.
skin	Organ used for protection and feeling.
slide	Glass sheet that a specimen is put on.
small intestine (in-test-in)	Organ used to digest and absorb food.
solar cells	Flat plates that transfer light energy into electrical energy.
solar eclipse	When the Moon is between the Sun and the Earth, and casts a shadow on part of the Earth.
solar panels	Flat plates that use the Sun's energy to heat water.
solar power	Generating electricity by using light or heat energy from the Sun.
solar system	A star with planets and other objects orbiting it.
solid	Something with a fixed shape and volume.
species (spee-shees)	A group of organisms that can reproduce with each other to produce offspring that will also be able to reproduce.
specimen (spess-im-men)	What you look at down a microscope.
speed	How fast something is moving. Often measured in metres per second (m/s).
sperm cell	The male sex cell.
sperm count	The number of sperm cells in a certain volume of semen. This is normally 20 million sperm per cm³.
sperm duct	Tube that carries sperm from the testes to the urethra.
sphere (sfear)	A shape like a ball.
stage	Part of the microscope. You put slides on it.
stain	Dye used to colour parts of a cell to make them easier to see.
star	A huge ball of gas that gives out heat and light energy.
states of matter	The three different forms that a substance can be in: solid, liquid or gas.
static electricity	A force which attracts things. It is caused when certain materials rub together.
stationary (stay-shun-arry)	Not moving.
stem	Plant organ used to take water to the leaves and to support the leaves.
stomach (stum-ack)	Organ used to break up food.
stopping distance	The distance a car moves while it is stopping. The stopping distance is equal to the thinking distance and the braking distance added together.
sulphuric acid (sull-fyour-ick)	A common acid. Used in car batteries.
Sun	The star that the Earth orbits.
sustainable	A way of living that does not use up non-renewable resources or harm things in our surroundings. Something that is sustainable allows things to continue into the future.
sweepnet	A net which is swept through long grass to catch tiny animals.
testis	Male reproductive organ. Produces sperm cells. Plural: testes.
test-tube baby	A baby that is produced using IVF.
texture	The scientific word used to describe the shapes and sizes of the crystals or grains in a rock.

theory (thear-ree)	A way of explaining why things happen as they do. A scientific theory can always be tested against the evidence (usually from experiments).
thinking distance	The distance a car travels while the driver is deciding to press the brake pedal.
thorax	Middle part of an animal's main body. In insects the legs are attached to the thorax.
tidal power	Generating electricity using the energy transferred from the tides.
tissue (tiss-you)	A group of the same cells all working together.
top predator	The last animal in a food chain.
total eclipse	A solar eclipse when the Moon completely blocks out light from the Sun.
trachea (track-ee-a)	More scientific name for windpipe.
transfer	To move from one place to another. For example, when a fuel burns, energy stored in the fuel is transferred to the thing being heated.
transport	The movement of rock grains and fragments by wind or water.
tree beating	Hitting the branches of a tree and collecting small animals that fall out.
ultrasound scan	An ultrasound scanner uses sound to create a picture of what is inside a body.
umbilical cord (um-bill-ick-al)	Carries food, oxygen and waste between the placenta and the growing foetus.
unbalanced forces	Two forces working in opposite directions that are not the same strength.
universal indicator	A mixture of indicators giving a different colour depending on how weak or strong an acid or alkali is.
Universe	All the galaxies and the space between them.
unstable	A chemical that can decompose very easily.
upthrust	A force that pushes things up in liquids and gases.
uranium (yer-rain-ee-um)	A fuel used in nuclear power stations.
urethra (you-ree-thra)	A tube carrying semen or urine running down the centre of the penis in males. A tube carrying urine in females.
uterus (you-ter-ous)	Organ in females in which a baby develops.
vacuole (vack-you-oll)	Storage space in plant cells.
vacuum (vack-yoom)	A completely empty space.
vagina (vaj-eye-na)	Tube in females. The penis is placed here during sexual intercourse.
variation	The differences between things.
vertebrate (vert-eb-rate)	An animal with a backbone.
voltage	A way of saying how much energy is transferred by electricity.
volume	The amount of room something takes up. Often measured in cubic centimetres (cm³).
water resistance	A force that tries to slow things down that are moving through water. It is a type of friction.
water transport system	Set of organs in a plant needed to carry water up the plant.
weight	The amount of force with which gravity pulls something towards the Earth. It is measured in newtons (N).
wind turbine	A kind of windmill that generates electricity using energy from the wind.
windpipe	Organ in the shape of a tube that takes air to and from your lungs.
word equation	A way of writing out what happens in a chemical reaction.
xylem tissue (zy-lem)	Found in roots, stems and leaves. Transports water. Made of xylem cells.
xylem cell (zy-lem)	Cell used to form tubes of xylem tissue.
year	The length of time it takes a planet to go around the Sun once. One year on Earth is 365.25 days.

Index